70119025

Plough Quarterly

BREAKING GROUND FOR A RENEWED WORLD

Winter 2017, Number 11

Artists: William Blake, Brigitta Racz, Zhu Jiuyang, Lukandwa Dominic, Christina Maendel, Bill Jacklin, Neil Welliver, Jason Landsel, Pino D'Amico, Piet Mondrian, William Johnson, John Noltner, Bob Bell

WWW.PLOUGH.COM

Plough Quarterly

WWW.PLOUGH.COM

Meet the community behind Plough.

Plough Quarterly is published by the Bruderhof, an international community of people seeking to follow Jesus together. Members of the Bruderhof are committed to a way of radical discipleship in the spirit of the Sermon on the Mount. Inspired by the first church in Jerusalem (Acts 2 and 4), members renounce private property and share everything in common in a life of service to God, one another, and neighbors near and far.

The community includes families and single people from a wide range of backgrounds, with around 2,700 people in all. There are twenty-three Bruderhof settlements in both rural and urban locations in the United States, England, Germany, Australia, and Paraguay.

To learn more or arrange a visit, see the community's website at *bruderhof.com.*

Plough Quarterly features original stories, ideas, and culture to inspire everyday faith and action. Starting from the conviction that the teachings and example of Jesus can transform and renew our world, we aim to apply them to all aspects of life, seeking common ground with all people of goodwill regardless of creed. The goal of *Plough Quarterly* is to build a living network of readers, contributors, and practitioners so that, in the words of Hebrews, we may "spur one another on toward love and good deeds."

Plough Quarterly includes contributions that we believe are worthy of our readers' consideration, whether or not we fully agree with them. Views expressed by contributors are their own and do not necessarily reflect the editorial position of Plough or of the Bruderhof communities.

Editors: Peter Mommsen, Sam Hine, Maureen Swinger. Art director: Emily Alexander. Online editor: Erna Albertz.
Founding Editor: Eberhard Arnold (1883–1935).
Plough Quarterly No. 11: Alien Citizens
Published by Plough Publishing House, ISBN 978-0-87486-039-9
Copyright © 2016 by Plough Publishing House. All rights reserved.

Scripture quotations (unless otherwise noted) are from the New Revised Standard Version Bible, copyright © 1989 the Division of Christian Education of the National Council of the Churches of Christ in the United States of America. Used by permission. All rights reserved.
Cover image from *obucheniezarubezhom.blogspot.com.* Inside cover image from *fineartamerica.com.*

Editorial Office	*Subscriber Services*	*United Kingdom*	*Australia*
PO Box 398	PO Box 345	Brightling Road	4188 Gwydir Highway
Walden, NY 12586	Congers, NY 10920-0345	Robertsbridge	Elsmore, NSW
T: 845.572.3455	T: 800.521.8011	TN32 5DR	2360 Australia
info@plough.com	subscriptions@plough.com	T: +44(0)1580.883.344	T: +61(0)2.6723.2213

Plough Quarterly (ISSN 2372-2584) is published quarterly by Plough Publishing House, PO Box 398, Walden, NY 12586.
Individual subscription $32 per year in the United States; Canada add $8, other countries add $16.
Periodicals postage paid at Walden, NY 12586 and at additional mailing offices.
POSTMASTER: Send address changes to *Plough Quarterly*, PO Box 345, Congers, NY 10920-0345.

STATEMENT OF OWNERSHIP, MANAGEMENT, AND CIRCULATION (Required by 39 U.S.C. 3685) 1. Title of publication: Plough Quarterly. 2. Publication No: 0001-6584. 3. Date of filing: September 30, 2016. 4. Frequency of issue: Quarterly. 5. Number of issues published annually: 4. 6. Annual subscription price: $32.00. 7. Complete mailing address of known office of publication: Plough Quarterly, P.O. Box 398, Walden, NY 12586. 8. Same. 9. Publisher: Plough Publishing House, same address. Editor: Peter Mommsen, same address. Managing Editor: Sam Hine, same address. 10. Owner: Church Communities Foundation, 2032 Rte 213, Rifton, NY 12471. 11. Known bondholders, mortgages, and other securities: None. 12. The purpose, function, and nonprofit status of this organization and the exempt status for federal income tax purposes have not changed during preceding 12 months. 13. Publication Title: Plough Quarterly. 14. Issue date for circulation data below: Fall 2015-Summer 2016. 15. Extent and nature of circulation: Average No. copies of each issue during preceding 12 months: A. Total number of copies (net press run)—12,000. B.1. Mailed outside-county paid subscriptions: 5,679. B.2. Mailed in-county paid subscriptions: 0. B.3. Paid distribution outside the mails including sales through dealers and carriers, street vendors, counter sales, and other non-USPS paid distribution: 127. B.4. Other classes mailed through the USPS: 0. C. Total paid distribution: 5,806. D.1. Free distribution by mail: Outside-county—717. D.2. In-county—0. D.3. Other classes mailed through the USPS—0. Free distribution outside the mail—644. E. Total free distribution: 1,361. F. Total Distribution: 7,167. G. Copies not distributed: 4,833. H. Total: 12,000. I. Percent paid—81.01%. Actual No. copies of single issue published nearest to filing date: A. 11,000. B.1. 5,101. B.2. 0. B.3. 113. B.4. 0. C. 5,214. D.1. 714. D.2. 0. D.3. 0. D.4. 654. E. 1,368. F. 6,582. G. 4,418. H. 11,000. I. 79.22%. Electronic copy circulation: Average No. copies of each issue during preceding 12 months: A. Total No. Electronic Copies: 172. B. Total paid print copies plus paid electronic copies: 5,978. C. Total paid print distribution plus paid electronic copies: 7,339. D. Percent paid: 81.45%. Actual No. copies of single issue published nearest to filing date: A. 147. B. 5,361. C. 6,729. D. 79.67%. 17. Publication of Statement of Ownership: Winter 2017. 18. I certify that the statements made by me above are correct and complete. Sam Hine, Editor, September 30, 2016.

Image from *en.tcgnordica.com*

Our Alien Citizenship

Dear Reader,

We may be heading for the fall of the West, former British foreign secretary William Hague recently warned. He was referring to November's unexpected election of Donald Trump to the US presidency and to the surge of populist nationalism around the globe. Hague's dismay is shared by many across the political spectrum. Even social conservatives who supported the Republican candidate for fear of a Democratic administration are bracing for turbulent years. Christian progressives lament a vote that both reflected and fueled an ugly turn in American politics – a defeat made bitterer by the knowledge that it was meted out by clear majorities of evangelicals, Protestants, and Catholics. Meanwhile, many of the working-class white voters who handed our next president the election feel that their security and identity are under threat.

It's a moment of anxiety when fear is understandable, even justified. But it is not Christian. The exhortation "Fear not" has served as the predictable springboard for a thousand Christmas sermons. It is also the gospel. As surely as a first-century Jew named Jesus is lord of the universe, God will have the last word on humankind's affairs. Who is in the White House should be as secondary a question to us as the rise of a new Roman emperor was to Peter and Paul.

On January 15, 1933, in the midst of the Great Depression, Dietrich Bonhoeffer preached to his Berlin congregation against the anxieties then engulfing Europe. For Christians, Bonhoeffer said, to live in fear is not acceptable: "Fear takes away a person's humanity. This is not what the creature made by God looks like. . . . The Bible, the gospel, Christ, the church, the faith – all are one great battle cry against fear in the lives of human beings." We who believe in Jesus must not fear, because we have heard the glad tidings of the arrival of a new political regime: the kingdom of God. We are patriots for a different homeland.

"Our citizenship is in heaven," the apostle Paul tells us (Phil. 3:20). Dorothy Day, the

Zhu Jiuyang, *Untitled.* Zhu Jiuyang, born in 1969, is a Christian artist working in mainland China.

New Yorker who founded the Catholic Worker movement, took his words literally: she never voted. Her reason, according to her friend Ammon Hennessy, was that she "did not bother to choose between the rival warmongers who sought to run the country," but "voted every day by practicing her ideals against war and the capitalist system which caused war."

Dorothy Day was anything but apolitical – she campaigned for women's suffrage and workers' rights, protested militarism, and struggled against racial injustices. Crucially, she did so not despite her faith but because of it. And it was for precisely the same reason that she took no part in electoral partisanship. She had a better, more lasting solution: to express in action Jesus' love to the oppressed, the vulnerable, and the guilty – to build up communities that embodied the kind of life that Jesus taught.

> **We must commit to the messy work of building up real flesh-and-blood church communities.**

Today more than ever, Day's kind of politics – the politics of an alien citizen – seems to make a lot of sense. This issue of *Plough* seeks to flesh out what it might look like to live accordingly. That's why we lead with an interview with Rod Dreher, whose proposal of what he calls the "Benedict Option" – a more communal Christianity – has sparked both wide interest and controversy (page 8).

For many, the first introduction to the early Christian vision of church community was the 1989 book *Resident Aliens* by Will Willimon and Stanley Hauerwas. On page 17, Willimon looks at what it means to be a resident alien today in light of an essay by Eberhard Arnold, Bonhoeffer's contemporary (page 22). Arnold's reflection, on the Incarnation and the church's calling to be the body of Christ in the world, helps us place contemporary questions within the great context in which they belong.

Arnold, like Bonhoeffer and Day, rejected the charge that Christian discipleship meant political quietism. On the contrary, he insisted that the church's mission has everything to do with the wider society:

> To be sure, the Christian is obliged to let himself be put to death rather than to instigate violent insurrection. All the more, he is challenged to combat oppression with every inner resource in the name of Jesus Christ. The Christian has the duty of standing up against all public or private wrong with power and commission and authority, even at the risk of death – just as was the case with John the Baptist and with Jesus himself.

As we face the radical uncertainties of the year ahead, may this fearlessness be ours as well.

Even more urgently, may we get to work building up the body of Christ on earth as a tangible sign of the justice of God's coming kingdom. This cannot remain just a topic for symposia and discussion groups. It means a commitment to the messy work of joining together in real flesh-and-blood church communities. It requires a new way of life.

As the angel told the shepherds of Bethlehem, the "glad tidings of great joy" with which we are entrusted will one day "be unto all peoples." Here, and nowhere else, is a politics to which we can rightly devote our lives and fortunes.

Warm greetings,

Peter

Peter Mommsen
Editor

Image from Wikimedia Commons (public domain)

On Joel Salatin's "Behold the Glory of Pigs," Autumn 2016: Without wishing to fall foul of Romans 14, I must say reading the last issue (and specifically Ronald Sider's and Joel Salatin's pieces together) made me wonder if a "consistent ethic of the sanctity of life" should not also be extended to the animals we share God's creation with? If we are going to allow them to "glory," as Joel helpfully puts it, should this also mean that we should stop killing and eating them?

Richard Barnard, Whitstable, Kent, UK

On John Dear's "Death Knell for Just War," Autumn 2016: If we cannot learn from scripture that Jesus was nonviolent, we can learn nothing about him, according to biblical scholar Fr. John L. McKenzie (1910–1991). Yet Jesus did not elaborate a theory and practice of nonviolence as John Dear claims. That would have to be left to a time when the material conditions were right, and that time is now.

How does John Dear explain Matthew 26:51, Luke 22:38, and John 18:10 if Jesus had taught a theory and practice of nonviolence? Matthew and Luke describe how one who accompanied Jesus to Gethsemane drew a sword and cut off the ear of the high priest's servant. Why had Jesus allowed one who walked with him to carry a sword? John identifies the swordsman as Peter, chief of the apostles, who had walked with Jesus throughout his entire public ministry. These fellows must have been very poor students if they had failed to absorb the theory and practice of nonviolence John Dear claims Jesus taught. Here the saying holds true: *Qui nimis probat, nihil probat.* He who tries to prove too much proves nothing.

The Catholic way is not *either/or* but *both/ and*. Not either just war categories or evangelical nonviolence, but both. Catholic teaching builds in continuity with the past rather than rupture. Do we really expect Pope Francis to teach, in effect, that our ancestors in the faith who held to just war theory were material heretics and that the Holy Spirit abandoned the church for 1,700 years until we pacifists came along? Don't count on it! You can count on a clear and forceful plea from Francis for a decisive turn to nonviolence in his anticipated encyclical – nonviolence using just war categories to determine the appropriate response to unjust war, the only kind possible in today's world.

Christian pacifists alone will not end the scourge of war. We must dialogue with Muslims, Jews, Hindus, Buddhists, and non-religious people of good will as well, and link arms in nonviolent resistance. In order to do so, we will have to use a mutually comprehensible language. In so doing we will inevitably reinvent the categories of just war theory, which are, after all, nothing more than tenets of the universal natural moral law.

Tom Cornell, Marlboro, NY

On "Forerunners: Muhammad Ali," Autumn 2016: Ali asserts that "We all have the same God, we just serve him differently." This is wrong on so many levels; I can't believe a "Christian" quarterly would offer it in praise of the man who spoke it. Ali is basically saying that the incarnation of Jesus, his death on the cross, and his resurrection are just unnecessary details, and that there is no mediator needed

Florence Fuller, *Inseparables*

between a holy God and unredeemed humanity. Does his supposed "love for humanity" accomplish what was necessary for Jesus to die to accomplish? Is there really "another way" after all, and Jesus did not need to drink from the cup the Father made him drink from?

Dave McCarty, West Milton, PA

On Shelley Douglass's "A World Where Abortion Is Unthinkable," Autumn 2016: Abortion is "thinkable" largely because it's legal. Infanticide remains taboo, but that could easily change if bioethicists like Peter Singer have their way. The late Richard John Neuhaus said it well: "Thousands of medical ethicists and bioethicists, as they are called, professionally guide the unthinkable on its passage through the debatable on its way to becoming the justifiable until it is finally established as the unexceptionable."

Michael Nacrelli, Clackamas, OR

On Sam Hine's "Gardening with Guns," Autumn 2016: I would appreciate it if you'd cancel my subscription. I receive a steady stream of "blame the gun" tripe from the news; I don't need to pay to have it delivered to my home as well. I understand the impulse to blame the tool as opposed to the person, but it's time to grow up and admit that some people are just plain evil. Utopia is a myth and some people who show a propensity for violence against their fellow man are irredeemable. We need to acknowledge this and quit blaming inanimate objects for the actions of those who wield them.   *Geoffrey Carlson, Coal City, IL*

On Erna Albertz's "Pursuing Happiness: How my sister with Down syndrome . . ." Autumn 2016: As a mother of two children with Down syndrome, I'm often amazed that my son, who has an IQ of 70, has more spiritual depth in a conversation than many with higher IQs. God gives to all gifts to be shared; if we see with God's eyes, we see the gifts others bring. I do believe this is realized in community. My two boys may not have a theological degree but they are grace and love incarnate – true followers of Jesus Christ.   *Lori Powell, Madison, WI*

Thoughts on Ploughing: I have been a reader of *Plough* for many years. To say that I have enjoyed every issue is simple truth but very inadequate. I look forward to each issue for the inspiration which it gives me in my ministry as a Catholic priest. While inspiring me, the *Plough* continues to disturb and to challenge me in my Christian commitment. The articles are all radical in the best sense of the word, because they are permeated by God's word and presumably reflect the lives of members of the Bruderhof communities. Thank you.

Desmond O'Donnell, Dublin, Ireland

What a powerful, enriching magazine! When I received my first copy two years ago here in prison, I knew I had an addiction – but a good one. Now there is wonderful news. I will be released from prison in ninety-seven days after five-and-a-half years. I will be back with my wife and grandkids. I guarantee I will continue my subscription to this fantastic magazine. Thank you sincerely.

Dennis Schaefer, El Mirage, AZ

We welcome letters to the editor. Letters and web comments may be edited for length and clarity, and may be published in any medium. Letters should be sent with the writer's name and address to letters@plough.com.

Image courtesy of Noah Filipiak

Remembering Muted Voices

The hundred-year anniversary of World War I has led many people to reflect on the staggering death and destruction caused by the "war to end all wars." It may be more helpful to consider the voices that spoke out and resisted this war. An upcoming symposium co-sponsored by *Plough* will remember a range of people who resisted World War I, from peace churches to suffragists, and the impact of their stories today. Speakers will include representatives of the American Friends Service Committee, the Fellowship of Reconciliation, the Hutterites, and the War Resisters League. Attendees will also have the opportunity to tour Fort Leavenworth and experience a memorial service for all conscientious objectors of World War I.

> **What:** Remembering Muted Voices: A Symposium on Conscience, Dissent, Resistance, and Civil Liberties in World War I and through Today
>
> **Where:** The National World War I Museum at Liberty Memorial, Kansas City, Missouri
>
> **When:** October 19–22, 2017

theworldwar.org/learn/remembering-muted-voices

A Book to Build Community

Noah Filipiak, a reader in Lansing, Michigan, wrote us to describe the impact that Plough's new title *Called to Community* is having among members of a Christian community development group in the city. He reports:

> We all live in the neighborhood and meet weekly at the garden project building in the park to discuss *Called to Community* [edited by Charles E. Moore, Plough, 2016]. The book's perspectives have been invaluable to us. Most of us are used to the typical American church model based on individualism. *Called to Community* has helped us see how most of the definitions we use for church today come from American values, not from biblical values. We all agree with these concepts, but it's a challenge to figure out how to apply them.

Similarly, Mark Smith began reading the book with a small group of friends near Philadelphia; their seeking is already developing into unanticipated forms of community:

> I'm finding that it's confirming what I already know to be true. We've been exploring the thought of living communally or as the early church. People have been called to this expression of faith for centuries, but what might be unique is the way or the magnitude in which it's happening today. It's exciting.

plough.com/calledtocommunity

The *Called to Community* discussion group in Lansing, MI

Poet in This Issue: Thomas Lequin

Thomas Lequin, whose poems "Testimony," "As For Me," and "Hanging On" appear in this issue, is a priest, farmer, fisherman, hunter, and Maine Master Guide. His poems have been published in *Anglican Theological Review, Iodine Poetry Journal, The Alembic,* and other journals, as well as in an anthology of contemporary animal poetry, *The Wildest Peal* (Moon Pie Press, 2015). ⤳

Building a Communal Church

Why the Benedict Option is Christianity's future – and how we get there

AN INTERVIEW WITH ROD DREHER

Norcia, Italy, the birthplace of Saint Benedict, whose monastic communities kept Christian culture alive during the Dark Ages

Previous spread: photograph by Pino D'Amico

How should Christians live as the society around us grows increasingly hostile to faith? *Plough's* Peter Mommsen visited the *New York Times*–bestselling author Rod Dreher in his Louisiana home for a wide-ranging conversation about Donald Trump, religious liberty, American empire, persecution – and why Christian community is a big part of the answer.

Peter Mommsen: *In recent months, you've created a stir by blogging about what you call the Benedict Option, and you have a forthcoming book by that title. What is the Benedict Option, and why do you think we need it?*

Rod Dreher: The name comes from Alasdair MacIntyre's 1981 book *After Virtue,* which compares our society's situation with the time after the fall of the Roman Empire. MacIntyre writes that we are waiting for a new and quite different Saint Benedict to teach us how to live in community again because we've become so fragmented. Benedict of Nursia was a young Christian born shortly after the fall of the Roman Empire who went to Rome to study. He became disgusted with the chaos and the decadence he saw in the city, and went out to the woods to pray and to ask God what he should do with his life. For three years he lived in a cave. When he came down, he founded a community of men to live together in what he called a school for the service of the Lord. This became the Benedictine order.

Benedict wrote his *Rule* as a constitution for these men to live together. That little document and Benedict's little

mustard-seed community of monks ended up becoming enormously influential in the life of the West. They held Christianity together during the so-called Dark Ages. The monks went into barbarian areas to evangelize, and if the barbarians killed them off, the mother house would send more brothers out. Slowly, these men laid the ground for the rebirth of Christian civilization in the West.

What does this have to do with us today? Although MacIntyre wasn't a Christian when he wrote his book, what I take from him is that we need small communities of committed believers who are willing to live counterculturally and bear witness. Christians today need to take stock of where we are as a culture and where we are likely to go. If our faith is going to make it over the generations, we are going to have to change our way of living dramatically. We're going to have to be much more intentional and much more communal.

Critics of the Benedict Option say that it's a form of retreat – of abandoning society in order to live a purer, holier life. Are they right to see a kind of selfishness in withdrawing?

Rod Dreher is a senior editor at The American Conservative *and the author of several books including the forthcoming title* The Benedict Option: A Strategy for Christians in a Post-Christian Nation, *to be released by Penguin in March 2017.*

Photograph by isahenderson

That's a claim that drives me crazy: "You just want to go run to the hills and live in your bunker and wait for the end." That's absolutely not what I'm saying. What I am saying is, we need to have a strategic, limited retreat from the mainstream for the same reason you would protect a candle with a lantern if you go outside in a gale. Otherwise, the wind would be so strong that it would blow the light out. The currents of culture have become so antithetical to Christianity that if we're going to form ourselves and our kids in the authentic faith, we're going to have to have some kind of limited withdrawal.

A gate in Norcia, Italy

What do I mean by that? I mean to put your kids in an authentic Christian school, for example. I mean things as simple as turning off the TV. Don't be so quick to open the door to popular culture. Growing up, I experienced how television wrecked any morals my parents were trying to teach us – they were fairly conservative, but the TV was like a sewer pipe into the home. Today it's smartphones. Even in my small Louisiana town, fifth-grade boys are watching hardcore pornography on their smartphones. The parents of these boys just choose not to see.

But it's not just running away from what's destructive – it's running toward something good. Our kids go to a classical school here in Baton Rouge. The teachers are trying to show the parents of the students: You may have the right instinct to get your kid out of the cesspit of the mainstream by sending them to this school, but it's not going to help if you just shelter them. You have to show them

something good and beautiful and true to build their souls up.

That's what I think the Benedict Option ideally should do. It should show the good fruits of a countercultural life in Christian community, and in that way be evangelical. If you're not evangelical in some sense you're not Christian. It is a missionary faith. But that doesn't mean that we have to throw ourselves in the middle of everything when we're not even properly formed. I know a lot of Christian parents don't want to take their kids out of the public schools because they say, "Well, our kids need to be salt and light." I'm afraid that's incredibly naïve in many cases, when you have third and fourth graders already talking about transgenderism and bisexuality.

The Benedictine monks set a good example here. They are much more cloistered than any lay community could afford to be. They say, "We have the walls there because we cannot fulfill our mission to serve Christ in the way we're called to serve him without some walls separating us from the world." But they also have a Benedictine principle of hospitality. Saint Benedict tells his monks to welcome every stranger and every visitor as Christ himself. That openness allows them to maintain contact with the world and to share the good things they have with the world.

For me as a member of the Bruderhof, the community that publishes Plough, *it's crucial that our life is not about withdrawal but precisely the opposite. Living in community is about building a place where the peace, justice, and love of the*

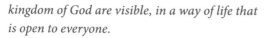

kingdom of God are visible, in a way of life that is open to everyone.

I agree. It's similar to when a husband and wife come together and pledge their lives to each other. They wall off the possibility of being involved romantically or sexually with anybody else so they can build something beautiful, deepen their love to each other and their love of God, and bring forth new fruit, that is to say, children. That is the attitude we need to have going into the Benedict Option.

Pope Benedict said that the greatest witness for the church is not its apologetics but the art it produces and its saints – the beautiful things that come out of its culture that reflect Christ and cause people to say, "God is in that." In the postmodern age, people don't really have the patience to hear rational arguments for the faith. Not to say we shouldn't make them, but they're going to be the least useful thing for spreading the faith. The most useful thing is going to be the love in our hearts and the good deeds and mercy that come out of that.

I remember when as a teenager – I was a very arrogant agnostic – I walked into the cathedral of Chartres in France. It knocked me flat. Nothing in my life had prepared me for the beauty of that medieval cathedral, the sense of harmony and depth. I knew that God was present. We don't even know who built the thing, but I knew this was built by people who knew God. I walked out of that church knowing that I wanted whatever inspired the men who built that cathedral.

We no longer live in the age of cathedral-building. But we Christians need to relearn the habit of making good art and not kitsch, which is the bane of church life. In the course of the Benedict Option, craftsmanship and artistry should be reborn out of these communities as a way of serving the world and as a way of witness.

We have to expand our sense of what evangelism is. Leading a person toward the sinner's prayer is one way of evangelizing. But another way I've found so effective with people I know who have come to the faith has been indirect: just being a friend to somebody, being open about your faith but not pushy, and living a life where the light of Christ shines through you.

That's what I found when I spent a week with the Benedictine monks in the monastery founded by Saint Benedict in what's now Norcia, Italy. The monks may never say a word to you about Jesus Christ, but you can see him in their faces, in the peace they have. I think that's going to be the most effective form of evangelization in the twenty-first century.

Faith in Public

You've written that Christianity is under assault in contemporary culture. But how real is the threat? Liberals argue, for instance, that Christian religious liberty claims are just a cover for persecuting LGBT folks.

They're wrong. In Canada right now there's a push among the medical community to deny doctors licenses and accreditation if they refuse to perform abortions or euthanasia. In Fort Worth, Texas, this past year, the superintendent tried to compel teachers to teach gender theory to elementary school kids – not call them boys or girls but call them "scholars" and "students." As a journalist at major newspapers in the 1990s, I was always "out" as a Christian, but today there's so much bias against Christians in American newsrooms that I don't think that would be possible. Where before my views on homosexuality – which are also my views on heterosexuality; I believe in the biblical standard – were just seen as eccentric, now they would probably keep me from being hired. The culture is slowly shifting to where people who affirm traditional Christian belief on sexuality are thought of as being morally equivalent to racists.

Many progressive Christians are saying: "We're sick of Christianity being a religion that is homophobic and obsessed with sexuality." But you've suggested that the sexual revolution is at the heart of the clash between the gospel and contemporary culture. Why is that?

Philip Rieff, a sociologist and a secular Jew, wrote a very important book in the sixties, *The Triumph of the Therapeutic*, in which he talked about the sexual revolution, which was just beginning, and he observed that opposition to sexual individualism is very near the core of Christian culture. Rieff said that since this opposition has not held, the churches will be discredited.

Jesus was a Jew of first-century Palestine; he believed and taught what Jews of that time believed about sexual purity. It's just stunning to me that we think we can just toss all that out now because we in the twenty-first-century West have decided we know better. If we say marriage can be whatever we want it to be and we can do whatever we want with our bodies, it doesn't matter as long as our hearts are OK with Jesus, we're throwing so much overboard that we can't throw overboard.

Russell Moore, a Southern Baptist leader, recently suggested that the marginalization of Christianity in the public square may be bad news for America but it's good news for the church. Would you agree?

Insofar as it purges the cultural Christianity from the church, I think it's good. On the other hand, there's going to be a lot of suffering ahead, and a lot of people on the margins of the church, who might have been gradually brought closer to Christ, are going to fall away. I can't rejoice in that or just say, "Bring it on," even though the purification will probably make the church stronger and more faithful in the end. When the Christian witness gets muted or pushed to the side, it's not just people in the church who will get hurt – society as a whole will suffer when it loses its leaven.

I think the church is going to have to become not more seeker-friendly but more finder-friendly. That means discipleship. We've got to go beyond just showing up on Sunday or having that altar-call conversion moment. What does it mean the next day? What does it mean to be formed in Christian habits, in Christian ways of life?

That's something the monks in Norcia teach. They showed me the value of routine, of saying the same prayers and psalms and getting the Bible into your heart by reading it daily in *lectio divina*. Those everyday, ordinary rhythms get the Christian faith into your bones. It's something we're going to have to recover if we're going to survive as a community of faith.

The Discipline of Community

As the Rule of Saint Benedict *makes clear, the kind of common life you're suggesting is impossible without discipline and mutual accountability.*

That's so necessary. I was talking to a Protestant pastor in Kentucky about this. A couple

> The monks may never say a word to you about Jesus Christ, but you can see him in their faces.

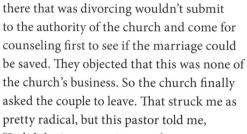

there that was divorcing wouldn't submit to the authority of the church and come for counseling first to see if the marriage could be saved. They objected that this was none of the church's business. So the church finally asked the couple to leave. That struck me as pretty radical, but this pastor told me, "It didn't give us any joy to ask this couple to leave. They were our brother and sister. But the community has to mean something. We have to have discipline or our faith is nothing but therapy, feeling good about things." It's similar for us in the Orthodox Church. The Orthodox pastors I've had take confession very seriously. They will not grant you communion if you don't come to regular confession and aren't accountable.

In American life, this kind of church discipline isn't something we're used to, but churches that don't discipline their members really aren't going to make it. The times I've grown spiritually have been when pastors or lay friends who were Christians called me to account and said, "You can't do this. If your faith really means something to you, you've got to change, you've got to repent."

That's an old-fashioned word we don't hear much in the church anymore: repent. But the Benedict Option is all about repentance, ongoing repentance. It's about realizing that we live in exile.

Are there ways that we as American churches have to repent?

Probably the worst thing we have to repent of as American Christians is lukewarmness: thinking of our faith as just something there for psychological comfort and to give us a general sense that God smiles on our middle-class American way of life. You can see now why so many young people are leaving the church – they were never given solid food.

We in the conservative church also have to repent of worshiping the nation, of nationalism, and of worshiping, to some degree, the Republican Party. For much of my life as an adult Christian, I never really stopped to think about how much of what I thought was true about Christianity was so consonant with the Republican view of the world. It wasn't until I had a child of my own that I began to think about the difference between what your generic Republican thought was the true and good way to live and the way that I as a Christian thought was the right way to live.

We have to repent of the politicization of church. Robert Putnam, in his book *American Grace,* found that, contrary to popular belief, the churches that are most politicized in their worship and sermonizing are progressive churches. So this is a problem for the whole church, not just the conservative churches. People on the left tend to focus on poverty, racism, and things like that, which are important. The conservatives tend to focus on abortion and sexuality. That's important too. I don't see many people in American Christianity doing a great job of integrating both. A friend of mine said the Democratic Party is a party of lust and the Republican Party is a party of greed, and both are deadly sins that Christians have to turn away from.

We also need to repent of ignorance – willful ignorance – of our past. At the start of modernity, the Enlightenment, we Westerners cut ourselves off from the Christian past and

> There's an old-fashioned word we don't hear much in the church anymore: repent.

said, "We're not fettered by any obligation to the past. We're going to be the authors of our own future." We don't like to acknowledge that the past has claims on us because that would inhibit our individual freedom. This is crazy! When you start reading about the history of the church and what our brothers and sisters in the faith went through to hold on to the gospel, it is appalling that we just turn our backs on our patrimony like that.

That's not to say that people in the past necessarily knew better than we do about all things; they didn't. There was never a golden age. But for heaven's sake, if we separate ourselves from our roots so thoroughly, we'll be carried off down the stream. We won't even know what it means to be a Christian anymore. That's what we're in danger of losing, the memory of what it has meant in the past to be a Christian. We need to hold on to that and steward it for our children and our children's children. If we don't have that sense, we're going to be completely assimilated by modernity. That's what's happening right now to too many Christians.

You wrote recently: "Our first loyalty is to the church, not to American empire. I want to encourage and cultivate faithful Christian resistance." That language is reminiscent of left-wing radicals such as Daniel Berrigan or Dorothy Day in their critique of American Christianity.

It is. I do not believe that political and theological conservatives have a monopoly on the truth. Look, I'm a conservative Christian. But we have been far too quick to think of the church as the Republican Party at prayer and to think of America as a new Israel. It's just not true. I love this country, which has been a tremendous blessing to me, but it's not a New Jerusalem. As Saint Augustine said, any peace we have today is going to be the peace of Babylon, of captivity.

I don't tell people not to be patriotic, but I do say, "Don't confuse patriotism with nationalism. Always remember that our first loyalty is to God and to Jesus Christ."

I was in New York on 9/11 – I was a columnist at the *New York Post* in downtown Manhattan when the towers fell. I became a vocal supporter of the Iraq War. At the time, I thought I was being very thoughtful, intelligent, and courageous, but in retrospect I realize I was just scared to death and was allowing myself to be manipulated by the government. We as the church have to be far more skeptical of what our government does.

What effect does the election of Donald Trump have on Christians' public witness? Does it change anything for the Benedict Option?

I was not a Trump voter, or a Clinton voter, and was prepared to be part of the loyal opposition no matter which candidate won. I still am. What does Trump's election change for the Benedict Option? Only this: I believe it gives us a bit more time to prepare – and, if he puts justices on the Supreme Court who value religious liberty, it gives us a little more space in which to prepare. But the idea that electing a Republican president, especially one as unchristian as Donald Trump, will arrest a cultural process of desacralization that has been underway for centuries – that's madness! I fear that Christians who were coming to appreciate the perilous position of the church in post-Christian America may conclude that we can all stand down now, that the danger has passed. That would be incredibly foolish. It's not simply the Democratic Party that threatens authentic Christianity. It's modernity. The best we can expect of politics is for it to open a space for the church to do its work of conversion and culture-building. The Trump presidency may – may – solve certain

immediate problems for the church, but it will certainly create new ones. Again, I say to my fellow Christians: do not take false hope from the machination of princes. Prepare.

Persecution Is Normal

In the last decade, more Christians may have been killed because of their faith than at any time since the sixteenth century. What is our responsibility to Christian brothers and sisters around the globe?

I asked a pastor who works with the persecuted church overseas the same question. He said that we Americans need to realize that what the persecuted church is suffering now has been the normative experience for most Christians through most of the life of the church, going back to the beginning; that what we're experiencing now in the West, this period of relative peace and non-persecution, is actually unusual. Persecution is normal. If we're not prepared to live that way if things turn bad in this country, then we're not worthy of the gospel. So I think we should be as supportive of them as we possibly can, but we also need to let their example of courage inform the way we prepare for what may be coming in our country.

In what may be dark times ahead, where do you see signs of hope, and what should we focus on to keep the joy of the gospel?

In my book, I write about a Catholic community in San Benedetto del Tronto, Italy, called the Tipiloschi – Italian for "the usual suspects." Although they go to the normal church, they also come together for communal meals, service projects, Bible study, communal prayer, and Mass every week. When I visited this community, I saw so much joy – not self-satisfied joy but creative joy. I met a couple of young men who had done prison time for minor offenses and now had been brought into

the community, given work to do, and rehabilitated. I went to their school, and saw such a sense of confidence. It's not a white-knuckle, we're-so-afraid-of-the-world approach. Because they know who they are in Christ, they live with joy. When I see people like that, I realize that this is not just some pipe dream or abstract ideal. There are flesh-and-blood people living this out right now.

I asked Marco Sermarini, who leads the Tipiloschi community, "Do you ever worry about anything?" He said, "Oh yes, Rod, I lie in bed at night and I worry about what's going to happen to my children and our community. But then I realize that our Lord came into Jerusalem on the back of a donkey, not a thoroughbred, and that I just have to be a donkey for the Lord." As long as we can be simple little donkeys, just plugging away doing the everyday ordinary things and sanctifying our everyday life, that's where we will find our hope.

This autumn, a terrible earthquake in Italy leveled the basilica of Saint Benedict in Norcia, rendering the monastery uninhabitable. By the grace of God, a couple of smaller earthquakes earlier in the fall had caused the monks to move to tents on the hill overlooking the town. Because they heeded the warnings of those earlier tremors, they survived the big one that destroyed both their basilica and all the churches in town. Now, despite their present suffering, they will be present for the rebuilding and are a sign of God's abiding presence among the people of Norcia.

The monks see a sign in all of this. So do I. Let those who have ears to hear hear what the Spirit is saying to the churches. ➤

Interview by Peter Mommsen on September 27 and November 9, 2016. ▶ *Watch the interview at* plough.com/dreher.

Artwork from a private collect on / Bridgeman Images

Bill Jacklin, *Calle II,* oil on canvas, 2008

Alien Citizens

WILL WILLIMON

Karl Barth, Eberhard Arnold, and Why the Church Is Political

In Resident Aliens, *their influential 1989 book, Will Willimon and co-author Stanley Hauerwas laid out a bracing vision of how to live Christianly in contemporary society. Where can Christians find guidance in the challenging times ahead? Plough asked the retired United Methodist bishop, now a Duke Divinity School professor, for his insights.*

What did Christians have at stake in the past presidential election? The question is not primarily which candidate we should have voted for, a decision that for me was made easy by Donald Trump. Instead, we ought to be asking: Why should we vote at all and, once the 55 percent of eligible voters have voted, what are Christians to make of the outcome of the election? How then shall we live now that "the people have spoken"?

How will Trump rule, or be led by those who want to rule through him? Now that less than half of the voters have coerced the rest of us to call Trump our leader, how then should we live? How will we exorcise the demon of American-style racism and xenophobia that Trump has unleashed?

For Christians, these questions, while interesting, are not the most pressing. Jesus' people participate uneasily in American democratic politics not because we are torn between the politics of the left and of the right, but because of the singular truth uttered by Eberhard Arnold in his 1934 sermon on the Incarnation: "Our politics is that of the kingdom of God" (see page 22).

Because Arnold was a man of such deep humility, peacefulness, and nonviolence, in reading his sermons it's easy to miss his radicality. How well Arnold knew and lived the oddness of being a Christian, a resident alien in a world where politics had become the functional equivalent of God. How challenging is Arnold's preaching in our world, where the political programs of Washington or Moscow can seem to be the only show in town, our last, best hope for maintaining our sense of security and illusions of control.

Christians carry two passports: one for the country in which we find ourselves, and another for that baptismal nation being made by God from all the nations. This nation is a realm not made by us but by God; Arnold calls it a "completely new order" where Christ at last "truly rules over all things."

As storm clouds gathered in Nazified Germany, and millions pinned their hopes on a political savior who would make Germany great again through messianic politics, Arnold defiantly asserted that the most important political task of the church was to join Paul in "the expectation, the assurance of a completely new order." How quaint, the world must have thought; how irrelevant Christian preachers can be.

Rather than offering alternative policies or programs to counter those of the Nazis, Arnold made the sweeping claim that "all political, all social, all educational, all human problems are solved in a concrete way by the rulership of Christ. This is what glory is."

About the same time as Arnold's sermon, Karl Barth was telling German preachers that they ought to preach "as if nothing happened." The "nothing" that they were to ignore was Hitler. Barth urged preachers not to waste pulpit time condemning the Nazis. Demons were on the prowl which could not be exorcized except through prayerful proclamation of the Word of God. Barth's famous Barmen Declaration (which never mentions Hitler) was a defiant statement that the church must be free to preach and that Christians listen intently to no other word than that of Jesus Christ. When the Nazis forced Barth to resign from his teaching position in Bonn, his last advice to his students bidding him a tearful farewell was to remain centered on scripture, exhorting them: "Exegesis, exegesis, exegesis!"

Were Barth and his friend Arnold escaping politics by not talking about politics? No. Arnold and Barth knew they were preaching God's word in a world where politics had purloined sacred rhetoric and assumed eternal significance for itself with talk of *Volk, Land, und Blut*. They talked politics but not as the world talks politics.

"We must deprive the politicians of their sacred pathos," Barth advised his fellow preachers. The flames of political zealotry must be starved by taking eternal significance off the table when we engage politics. The preacher must view the pretentious modern nation-state and its presumptive politics through a wide-angle lens. Politicians must not be allowed to assume a messianic posture, and citizens must be warned against giving politicians glory that belongs only to God. In other words, Barth and Arnold were determined to do politics in a peculiarly Christian way by talking about who God is and what God is up to before making any assessment of human alternatives to God.

God's Politics: The Body of Christ

Asked by *The Christian Century* to respond to the twenty-fifth anniversary of my book with Stanley Hauerwas, *Resident Aliens: Life in the Christian Colony*, a dozen reviewers dismissed the book as politically irrelevant, sectarian escapism from the great issues of the day. None noticed that the book was meant to address the church, not the US Senate. *Resident Aliens* was a work of ecclesiology that assumed that

when Christians are pressed to "say something political," our most faithful response is church. As Hauerwas famously puts it, the church doesn't have a social policy; the church *is* God's social policy.

Many of our critics showed that they still live under the Constantinian illusion that the United States is roughly synonymous with the kingdom of God. Even though the state alleges that it practices freedom of religion, the secular state tolerates no alternatives to its sovereignty. Christians are free in American democracy to be as religious as we please as long as we keep our religion personal and private.

Contemporary secular politics decrees that people of faith must first jettison the church's peculiar speech and practices before we can be allowed to go public and do politics. Many mainline Protestants, and an embarrassing number of American evangelicals, cling to the hope that by engagement with secular politics within the limits set by the modern democratic state, we can wrest some shred of social significance for the Christian faith. That's how my own United Methodist Church became the Democratic Party on its knees.

Saying it better than we put it in *Resident Aliens*, Arnold not only sees Christ as

> Christians carry two passports: one for the country in which we find ourselves, and another for that baptismal nation being made by God from all the nations.

Will Willimon's most recent book is Fear of the Other: Thinking Like Christians about Xenophobia *(Abingdon). This March his new book* Who Lynched Willie Earle? Confronting Racism through Preaching *will be published by Abingdon.*

"embodied in the church" but calls the church to go beyond words and engage in radical, urgent action that forms the church as irrefutable, concrete proof that Jesus Christ really is Lord and we are not: "Only very few people in our time are able to grasp the this-worldly realism of the early Christians. . . . Mere words about the future coming of God fade away in people's ears today. That is why embodied, corporeal action is needed. Something must be set up, something must be created and formed, which no one will be able to pass by," on the basis of our knowledge of who God is and where God is bringing the world. Our hope is not in some fuzzy, ethereal spirituality. "It takes place now, through Christ in the church. The future kingdom receives form in the church."

> **The most world-changing, revolutionary statement we can make is that Jesus reigns; that God, not nations, rules the world.**

In his sermon, Arnold eschews commentary on current events, as well as condemnation or commendation of this or that political leader, and instead speaks about the peculiar way Christ takes up room in the world and makes his will known through the ragtag group of losers we dare to call, with Paul, the very body of Christ. "It is not the task of this body of Christ to attain prominence in the political power structure of this world. . . . Our politics is that of the kingdom of God."

Because of who God is and how God works, the congregation where I preach, for all its failures (and I can tell you, they are many) is, according to Arnold, nothing less than "an embassy of God's kingdom": "When the British ambassador is in the British embassy in Berlin, he is not subject to the laws of the German Reich. . . . In the residence of the ambassador, only the laws of the country he represents are valid."

Arnold's sermon is a continually fresh, relevant rebuke to those who think we can do politics without doing church. Among many pastors and church leaders, there is a rather docetic view of ministry and the church. We denigrate many of the tasks that consume pastoral ministry – administration, sermon preparation, and congregational leadership – because we long to be done with this mundane, corporeal stuff so we can soar upward to higher, more spiritual tasks. Arnold wisely asserts Incarnation and unashamedly calls upon his congregants to get their hands dirty by engaging in corporate work: to set up, create, form, and learn all those organizational skills that are appropriate for an incarnational faith where we are saved by the Eternal Word condescending to become our flesh.

Preachers as Politicians

In Charleston, South Carolina, the senior pastor of Emanuel AME Church, Clementa C. Pinckney, was a state senator and a powerful politician. But the night he was martyred he was in the basement hall of his church, leading a small group of laypeople in prayer and Bible study. Much of the ordinary, unspectacular work pastors do is holy if we believe that the church is the incarnate Christ's chosen means of showing up in the world. Even the mundane body work done by pastors and lay leadership is sacred when it equips Christ's commissioned "ambassadors" and constitutes an "embassy" of another sovereignty, a living, breathing Body, something that a young South Carolina racist recognized as a threat to his white supremacist world.

The people who got the nation's attention by giving so bold a witness to forgiveness after the massacre at Mother Emanuel didn't drop down out of heaven. They were produced here on earth, in lifetimes of listening to sermons by pastors like Pinckney who took seriously their responsibility "to equip God's people for the work of serving" (Eph. 4:12).

I know a pastor who began his sermon after the Charleston massacre by asking, "How come our Bible studies in this church have not been truthful enough, intense enough, for anybody to want to kill us? Church, we need to figure out how to be so faithful in our life together that the world can look at us and see something that it is not. Our little congregation is called to be a showcase of what a living God can do!"

Christians are "political" because beliefs, including religious beliefs, have political consequences. However, Arnold's Incarnation sermon is based upon more than that hackneyed, common-sense observation. Arnold assumes that, when storm clouds gather and politicians strut their stuff before adoring audiences, the most world-changing, revolutionary statement we can make is that Jesus reigns; that God, not nations, rules the world; and that even the best of Caesar's solutions fall short of the kingdom of God. God's peculiar answer to what's wrong with the world, God's exemplification of creative social alternatives, is the church. These sweepingly political claims are more than personal and private. As Arnold says, because we know, through Christ, who God (i.e., reality) is, we "cannot shed blood or tolerate private property," we "cannot lie or take an oath," and we must uphold "the faithfulness between a man and woman in a marriage under the church," because we believe that God, not politics, names what's really going on.

Returning from a Moral Monday demonstration in Raleigh, North Carolina, where hundreds of us had gathered to once again castigate the state's political buffoons, I was rather pleased with myself for my courageous (though not costly) political activism. We got them told.

Listening to the radio on the way back, we heard Governor McCrory dismiss our demonstration as "just a bunch of aging hippies from the sixties." Ouch! Our Trump-wannabe governor bragged that polls showed close to 60 percent support for his right-wing policies.

"Preacher," said the person I had dragged to Moral Monday with me, "sounds like we don't need better politicians; we need a better class of voters. Maybe you should stay home and work on your Sunday sermon rather than get arrested in Raleigh."

I have met the political enemy, and he is . . . me and my fellow Christians, who find it so hard to embody our convictions, and who, even in our left-wing protests, unintentionally give credence to political scoundrels. If we are going to worship a Savior who is determined to tabernacle among us, to show up and thereby disrupt our settled arrangements with Caesar, then we can't avoid the mundane, corporeal work of having meetings, forming a congregation that becomes in its life together and its way in the world a visible, breathing, undeniable bodily presence of Christ.

That's why maybe my most radical, politically significant act is to take Eberhard Arnold as my model: stand up this Sunday and preach that God's will be done, God's reign will come on earth as in heaven, whether we like it or not. ➤

William Blake, *The Christ Child Asleep on a Cross,* tempera on canvas, 1799–1800

Artwork from Victoria & Albert Museum, London / Bridgeman Images

Becoming Flesh and Blood

EBERHARD ARNOLD

The Church and Its Dangerous Politics

How should the church relate to politics? There are
moments when this perennial question becomes suddenly urgent.
In August 1934, eighteen months after Hitler's rise to power, Eberhard
Arnold spoke to members of his community, the Bruderhof, whose
German branch had already been raided twice by Nazi forces. For them,
Christian witness to the state was no longer just theory.

Arnold's address had personal poignancy: among his listeners was
his eighteen-year-old nephew Hermann, until recently an enthusiastic
Nazi and member of the Storm Troopers. But Hermann had just experienced a conversion, requesting baptism and announcing that he would
take the risky step of publicly repudiating Nazism. Eberhard set out to
explain to the young man what kind of Reich (kingdom) he was signing
up for by becoming part of the church of Jesus Christ.

IT IS AN IMMENSELY WONDERFUL THING when a human
heart is touched and moved by God. This is something only God can do;
no human has this power, as truly as God is God. For no one knows the
thoughts of God except for God's own Spirit (1 Cor. 2:11).

The only human being able to show what is in God was himself born
of the Holy Spirit: Jesus. The manner in which his birth through Mary
took place is the unique sign and example for how every new
birth from the Spirit takes place. The Spirit came to Mary. Mary
believed, and received the living Word of God. Because she had
faith, the Word took flesh and form from her.

Today too the living Word wants to take human form: the
eternal Christ wants to have a body. It is for this that the Holy
Spirit is sent from the throne of the Father and of the Son. And this
is why Christ broke down the barriers and walls through his cross – so that his
new embodiment, his new manifestation among humankind, might come into
being: the church (Eph. 2:14–16).

Just as the eternal, living Word once took on a body as Mary's son, so today
it becomes flesh anew in the church. This is what the apostle means when he
writes that a "mystery" has been entrusted to him, the mystery of the body of
Christ (Col. 1:24–26). What does it mean that the church is Christ's body? In the
church, Christ receives a physical form that makes him visible and tangible in
the world – otherwise the word *body* would be meaningless. (Theologians who
speak of an invisible body of Christ only prove that there is a kind of nonsense of
which theologians alone are capable. The apostles did not believe in ghosts.)

> In the church,
> Christ receives a physical
> form that makes him
> visible and tangible in
> the world.

The Embodied Church

In the Letter to the Colossians, the apostle describes how this process of becoming visible is made manifest in the church. He speaks of "the mystery" of the body of Christ, "which is Christ in you"; and secondly, he speaks of the expectation of Christ's future coming in majesty – the "hope of glory" (Col. 1:27).

Just as Christ was in Mary, so Christ is in us who believe and love.

These phrases have become so trite that they no longer convey anything to us. To experience their power, we must translate them into the language of today. "Hope" in the New Testament is the expectation and assurance of a completely new order. "Glory" means Christ's majesty following his accession to the throne. This is the glory: that God, through Christ, now truly rules over all things. It means that all political, social, educational, and human problems are solved in a concrete way by the rulership of Christ. This is what glory is.

Only very few people in our time are able to grasp the this-worldly realism of the early Christians. It is in this realistic sense that the Word of God, Christ, is to become embodied in the church. Mere words about the future coming of God fade away in people's ears today. That is why embodied, corporeal action is needed. Something must be set up, something must be created and formed, which no one will be able to pass by.

"Christ in you" is the first part of this mystery. Just as Christ was in Mary, so Christ is in us who believe and love. When this is the case, we live in a particular way. The character of our conduct in our daily lives shows forth the character of God's future. This is not a matter of moralistic effort or juristic fiat; it is something organic. It takes place now, through Christ in the church. In the church, his future kingdom receives form.

This is the reason why the church lives in perfect peace and perfect justice, and why it cannot shed blood, tolerate private property, speak a lie, or take an oath (Matt. 5–7). This is also why the church cannot tolerate the destruction of bridal purity, that is, of the faithfulness between a man and woman in a marriage under the church.

For the same reason, the church must remain free of all actions by which human beings are made great. The church lives for one purpose: that God may bring everything under his rule on the throne of his kingdom. Thus in the church there can be no idolatry of human beings; no one should imagine that this or that individual is a second or a third or fourth Christ. Christ's body, his new incarnation, is not the individual believer, but rather the church in the entirety of its corporeal life.

Through its work in the natural world, the believing church community molds physical things in accordance with the simpleness and singleness of Christ. Great art is simplicity of line. So too, the simplest life is the most beautiful. Closeness to nature – to the world created by God – gives freedom

William Blake, *The Nativity*, tempera on copper, 1799–1800

In this symbolic painting showing the miraculous significance of Jesus' birth, Joseph supports Mary while her child springs forth into the world. He is welcomed by Mary's cousin Elizabeth, whose own child, John the Baptist, rests in her lap. A cross glows in the window as if reflected in the light of the star of Bethlehem.

Artwork from Philadelphia Museum of Art, Pennsylvania. Gift of Mrs. William Thomas Tonner, 1964 / Bridgeman Images

from all unnaturalness and artificiality. This is why the work done in the church community ought to be in keeping with the simplicity of Christ, for example architecture and tableware. By the same token, voluntary poverty belongs to the embodiment of Christ, especially if it arises out of love. Because we as the church are called to serve the whole world, especially those in need, we must live as simply as possible in order to help as many people as we can.

The Church's Politics

It is a widespread error to mix this specific task of the church with public affairs. As Paul shows very clearly, the church, with its task of being the embodiment of Christ, is thrust in among the nations as a unique anticipatory presence which points forward to the coming of the kingdom on earth (Col. 3:1–4; Eph. 1:9–14). Accordingly, it is not the task of the body of Christ to attain prominence in the political power structure of this world (1 Cor. 1:26–29; 2:6–8; 2 Cor. 4:7–10).

Thus, according to the apostolic teaching, there is no such thing as a Christian state. A Christian church fights neither for the interests of the state nor against them. No head of a state can legitimately wield the sword in the name of Christ, and no church is permitted to bless any attempts to do so. Nor can there be a "Christian politics" in international organizations such as the League of Nations. If the League of Nations decides to organize an armed punitive police force, no one can rightly claim that this is done in the name of Christ.

There are two distinct and separate spheres of life: one is the state and the other is the church. National or international politics are not the Christian's politics. The apostle says that our politics is in heaven, from where we expect our Lord Jesus Christ to come (Phil. 3:20). Our politics is that of the kingdom of God.

Therefore, beloved Hermann Arnold, I want to entrust you with the very highest and greatest thing which can exist for a human being. You are asked whether you can take upon yourself the task of serving the church in its mission as an embassy of God's kingdom. The apostle Paul says we are ambassadors of the kingdom of God (2 Cor. 5:18–20). One must understand this statement in the sense of diplomacy. When the British ambassador is in the British Embassy in Berlin, he is not subject to the laws of the German Reich. The grounds of the embassy are inviolable: in the residence of the ambassador, only the laws of the country he represents are valid.

> We are ambassadors of the reign of God. This means that we do nothing at all except what the King of God's kingdom would do.

Paul says that we are ambassadors of God, representing Christ, the Messiah King, the regent of that last kingdom – a kingdom represented not by any state or government of this world, but rather by the church. We are ambassadors of the reign of God. This is something enormous. It means that we do nothing at all except what the king of God's kingdom would himself do for his kingdom. And the will of this king is to unite. This is why the apostle says we are God's ambassadors on behalf of Christ, appealing to all people, "Be reconciled to God." Our task is reconciliation and uniting, and nothing else. There is nothing else we have to do in this world.

When we take this service upon ourselves we enter into mortal danger. Whoever goes the way of Christ goes the way of the cross, for the world, the state, and society are not willing to follow such a call. Nevertheless, there is in every human heart the certainty that this is the only way of truth. As Paul writes, our testimony will bear witness to every human conscience that it is the truth (Rom. 2:15; 2 Cor. 4:2). This conviction gives us the courage of love, because we sense that what we are proclaiming is what all our fellow human beings want as well. At the moment, to be sure, they feel unable to begin this way because they are hypnotized, under a spell, and subject to the power of suggestion. Yet they themselves sense that God's peace and justice is the way the world should be!

There is no greater bravery than that of faith. There is no greater courage than that of love.

Reconstructed from a transcript of Eberhard Arnold's address to the Alm Bruderhof, Principality of Liechtenstein, on August 3, 1934 (Bruderhof Historical Archive, EA 255). Translated by Nicoline Maas.

Painting from varesenews.it/blog

THOMAS NAUERTH

Finding Utopia

Utopia, *the famous book by the martyr Thomas More, is five hundred years old this year. The yearning for utopia has had an immense impact on history – sometimes for good, often for ill. But should we be so quick to dismiss More's vision of a society free of violence and private property?*

ON OCTOBER 31 of this year, Pope Francis and the Lutheran Archbishop of Sweden joined together in an ecumenical service to commemorate the start of the Reformation 499 years ago. As the international media coverage made clear, there is good reason to mark this date: what happened after Martin Luther posted his ninety-five theses on

Sergio Michilini, *The Island of the Living,* (detail) 1995

the church door in Wittenberg in 1517 ended up transforming Europe and the world, triggering conflicts that tore apart church and society. The century of bloody religious warfare that followed laid the groundwork for the modern nation-state system and the rise of secularism.

While these geopolitical developments garner much attention, other aspects of the sixteenth century have largely disappeared from view. And yet these neglected histories cast light on questions that are just as urgent today as they were a half-millennium ago. For example, take the first question of all: How should we live? At the beginning of the sixteenth century, this question erupted throughout Europe. People began asking: How should we structure our society? How can we provide justice, peace, and equality for all?

When such questions are raised, it indicates that people's thought-world has changed. All of a sudden they realize that customary practices, things that have always been done a certain way, might actually be improved or abandoned. People gain the ability to look at their own situation from the outside, to analyze their own way of life. Specifically, they become able to take a hard look at how the basic assumptions of their society measure up against the Christian gospel.

It was in this sense that sixteenth-century Europeans saw the basics of their faith with fresh eyes. They sought to identify what was essential to living as a Christian. In their writings and publications, they sparked a continent-wide conversation about fundamentals among educated readers and thinkers.

The sixteenth-century movement that grew out of this new ability to look critically at conventional ways of living is known as humanism. Among its most prominent champions was the English jurist Thomas More, whose masterwork *Utopia* was published five hundred years ago this year. (Now canonized as a Catholic saint, More may be most widely known thanks to the Academy Award–winning film *A Man for All Seasons*, which portrays his martyrdom in 1535 at the hands of King Henry VIII.)

Written in Latin, *Utopia* is a philosophical dialogue in the form of a short story that has been called "one of the most interesting pieces of political literature ever written." [1] The book reflects the many conversations that More shared with his fellow humanists, especially his close friend Erasmus of Rotterdam.

While *Utopia* is the title under which the work is best known – More's neologism would spawn a whole new literary genre of utopias – the book's original title is considerably longer, and hints at More's real interest: *On the Best State of a Republic and the New Island Utopia.* While containing abundant social satire, the book's aim is ultimately to invite readers to reflect: How can society function better than it does now?

The narrative's literary structure is sophisticated. Near the end of the first part of the book, the narrator, known to the reader as "Thomas More," describes meeting a foreign sailor while on a business trip to Flanders on behalf of the king of England. The sailor's name is Raphael Hythlodeus. The two new acquaintances begin a wide-ranging conversation about England's and the Continent's political situation. Raphael then remarks:

> To speak plainly my real sentiments, I must freely own that as long as there is any property, and while money is the standard of all other things, I cannot think that a nation can be governed either justly or happily: not justly,

Dr. Thomas Nauerth is a professor of Catholic theology at the University of Osnabrück, Germany.

Images from Wikimedia Commons (public domain)

Left, Hans Holbein the Younger, *Sir Thomas More,* 1527
Right, The Island of Utopia, colorized version of a woodcut in Thomas More's *Utopia,* 1516

because the best things will fall to the share of the worst men; nor happily, because all things will be divided among a few (and even these are not in all respects happy), the rest being left to be absolutely miserable.[2]

Is it not remarkable how these sentences from the sixteenth century speak directly to today's social and political debates? I only need remind the reader, for example, of French economist Thomas Piketty's 2014 book *Capital in the Twenty-First Century* and the controversy it has sparked. These same concerns occupy More's mysterious stranger, who continues:

> When I reflect on the wise and good constitution of the Utopians, among whom all things are so well governed and with so few laws, where virtue hath its due reward, and yet there is such an equality that every man lives in plenty – when I compare with them so many other nations that are still making new laws, and yet can never bring their constitution to a right regulation . . . where, notwithstanding everyone has his property, yet all the laws that they can invent have not the power either to obtain or preserve it, or even to enable men certainly to distinguish what is their own from what is another's, of which the many lawsuits that every day break out, and are eternally depending, give too plain a demonstration.

The historical Thomas More was a lawyer. From his professional life, he was all too familiar with the ways in which "many lawsuits" could be a symptom of deep problems in a country's legal system. This minor observation highlights an ambiguity that runs throughout the book: it's far from clear that the "Thomas More" whom we meet in the pages of *Utopia* is identical to the real Thomas More. After all, here it is the foreign sailor Raphael who is giving voice to the real More's professional experiences. Yet in the book, the character "Thomas More" at times disagrees with Raphael's opinion.

Why might the character "Thomas More" express views different from those of the real Thomas More? We must remember that the author was living in the dangerous political climate of sixteenth-century England, in which the risk of losing one's head was all too real. Thus, it must have been highly expedient for him that his fictional namesake decisively rejected Raphael's argument for total community of goods. This pattern repeats itself throughout the book. Whenever *Utopia* touches on politically sensitive subjects, the author sends the character "Thomas More" into the field to disavow anything that might seem subversive. It's a device that allows him to safeguard both his creative and his physical liberty.

It is for this reason, perhaps, that at the end of the first part of *Utopia* the character "Thomas More" criticizes Raphael's suggestion that private property is the root of all evil:

> "On the contrary," answered I, "it seems to me that men cannot live conveniently where all things are common. How can there be any plenty where every man will excuse himself from labor? For as the hope of gain doth not excite him, so the confidence that he has in other men's industry may make him slothful."

The foreign sailor shows great understanding for the fictitious "Thomas More's" objection, but responds confidently on the basis of his own experience:

> "I do not wonder," said Raphael, "that it appears so to you, since you have no notion, or at least no right one, of such a constitution; but if you had been in Utopia with me, and had seen their laws and rules, as I did, for the space of five years, in which I lived among them,

and during which time I was so delighted with them that indeed I should never have left them if it had not been to make the discovery of that new world to the Europeans, you would then confess that you had never seen a people so well constituted as they."

ARE YOU SLOWLY growing curious about the commonwealth of Utopia? If so, then the refined literary strategy of the author Thomas More has caught you in its grip. The function of the entire first part of the book is to use contemporary political and social problems to make the reader hungry for more information about this alternative society. The book's second part then offers answers that have much to say not just to the sixteenth century, but to the twenty-first as well.

Here we find a portrait of a totally different and new society: a "no place" (Greek *ou-topos* in a literal sense) but certainly also a "good place" (*eu-topos*). This society is not a Christian one. (No doubt this point was politically helpful to the real Thomas More, allowing him to disavow his book as a mere fantasy.) Nevertheless, we are confronted with "the paradigmatic and congenial draft plan of a society of community of property, which will more or less have an impact on all other considerations."[3]

Utopian society, we learn, is made up of communities of families who renounce money and private ownership. Markets do exist but are organized according to unfamiliar principles:

> Every city is divided into four equal parts, and in the middle of each there is a market-place. What is brought thither, and manufactured by the several families, is carried from thence to houses appointed for that purpose, in which all things of a sort are laid by themselves; and thither every father goes, and takes whatsoever he or his family stand in need of, without

either paying for it or leaving anything in exchange. There is no reason for giving a denial to any person, since there is such plenty of everything among them; and there is no danger of a man's asking for more than he needs; they have no inducements to do this, since they are sure they shall always be supplied. . . . No man is poor, none in necessity, and though no man has anything, yet they are all rich.

Naturally, Utopia also boasts an elaborate system of hospitals and nursing care. In general, it is a society that defines wealth differently than we do:

What can make a man so rich as to lead a serene and cheerful life, free from anxieties; neither apprehending want himself, nor vexed with the endless complaints of his wife? He is not afraid of the misery of his children, nor is he contriving how to raise a portion for his daughters; but is secure in this, that both he and his wife, his children and grand-children, to as many generations as he can fancy, will all live both plentifully and happily.

Having sketched out this daring vision, how does the author Thomas More conclude his *Utopia*? Unsurprisingly in view of his literary approach, he leaves the book open-ended, forcing readers to make up their own minds. After Raphael finishes his narrative account, the character "Thomas More" offers this sphinx-like conclusion:

When Raphael had thus made an end of speaking, though many things occurred to me, both concerning the manners and laws of that people, that seemed very absurd, as well in their way of making war, as in their notions of religion and divine matters – together with several other particulars, but chiefly what seemed the foundation of all the rest, their living in common, without the use of money. . . . In the meanwhile, though it must be confessed that he is both a very learned man and a person who has obtained a great knowledge of the world, I cannot perfectly agree to everything he has related. However, there are many things in the commonwealth of Utopia that I rather wish, than hope, to see followed in our governments.

WHEN THOMAS MORE wrote these words in 1516, he could not have known how differently the sixteenth century would turn out from what he and his fellow humanists hoped. After 1517, as the phenomenon that would later be called the Reformation got underway, their high-minded discussions, anchored in a shared commitment to reason, gave way to bitter doctrinal disputes.

Yet the Reformation was by no means a monolithic or uniform movement – a fact that is often overlooked. It was, on the contrary, colorfully diverse. By 1525 at the latest, when the Anabaptist movement arose in Ulrich Zwingli's Zurich, it would be more accurate to speak of Reformations in the plural. In an intriguing parallel to the humanist movement of Erasmus and More, the radical wings of the Reformation were far less concerned with doctrine than with how human life was to be lived.

Though subject to horrific persecution almost immediately after it emerged, the Anabaptist movement gave rise to a way of life remarkably close to the social vision described by Thomas More. Jakob Hutter, an Anabaptist from Tyrol, developed a communal church that rejected all private property. According to Grete Mecenseffy, an authority on Hutter and his movement, "the decisive issue for him was the organization of communal life, the establishment of production and consumer cooperatives known as *Haushaben* or *Bruderhöfe*."[4] These communal groups found refuge

From a collection in the Central Library of Zurich, obtained from Heinold Fast

Sixteenth-century paintings show an illicit Anabaptist meeting followed by the arrest of two Anabaptist preachers.

in Moravia and grew rapidly, consisting of over ten thousand people in about forty-two Bruderhofs by 1600. These communities had "a comprehensive and diversified organization both in spiritual and in economic matters." [5]

As prophesied in *Utopia,* according to the report of an eyewitness: "No one was idle, everyone was busy doing what he was told . . . just like the inner workings of a clock." [6] During their golden years, the Hutterite communities were economically successful, demonstrating that the Utopian ideals of Raphael Hythlodeus (or of Thomas More?) were not merely "utopian" after all. After centuries of on-and-off persecution in Europe, the Hutterites immigrated to North America in 1877. They established three colonies then; today about 550 Hutterite communities exist in the United States and Canada, home to more than seventy thousand souls.

In addition to community of goods, the Hutterites are also characterized by an uncompromising commitment to peace. Based on their understanding of the gospel, they, like most Anabaptists, strictly reject any participation in violence. Notably, the rejection of violence seems to go hand in hand with the rejection of property. In *Utopia* too – though it never appeals to Christian scripture – the communitarian life, free of property, is linked to a strong commitment to peace. As Raphael Hythlodeus describes it:

> They detest war as a very brutal thing, and which, to the reproach of human nature, is more practiced by men than by any sort of beasts. They, in opposition to the sentiments of almost all other nations, think that there is nothing more inglorious than that glory that is gained by war. . . . They reckon that a man acts suitably to his nature when he conquers his enemy in such a way as that no other

creature but a man could be capable of, and that is by the strength of his understanding.

Could there have been a direct connection between *Utopia* and the ideas of Jakob Hutter?[7] We can only speculate. In any case, the tracks of Erasmus can be traced among the early Anabaptists, and education played a major role in the Hutterite communities, as was the case among the Utopians.

SOME OF THE EARLIEST descriptions of Hutterite life come from the pen of one Christoph Andreas Fischer, a Jesuit. To say that he was not a fan of theirs would be an understatement. One of his polemical tracts against the Hutterites, written in 1607, is titled "What the Anabaptists think of the community of goods: must all possessions be shared in common?"[8] He answers, of course, with a resounding negative.

Fischer's sharp criticism of communal living is particularly interesting because at exactly this time, his fellow Jesuits were launching another "communistic" experiment in South America. Just as with Hutterite communities, this was a utopia that sprang out of troubled circumstances.[9] The indigenous Americans, for whom the Jesuit missionaries felt a pastoral responsibility, had been oppressed and enslaved by the Spanish conquistadors. In response, in 1600 the Jesuits began to organize them into large communities that, thanks to their status as Jesuit settlements, were promised freedom from persecution and slavery. These settlements were not individual estates, but large social structures that became known as "Jesuit Missions," as memorably portrayed in Roland Joffé's 1986 film *The Mission*. Like the Hutterite colonies, they were an explicitly "communistic-theocratic experiment,"[10] one that survived for more than one-and-a-half centuries until their suppression in 1768.

In a total of thirty-one villages, called *reducciones,* lived more than a hundred thousand indigenous people with around one hundred and fifty Jesuits. All non-Jesuit Europeans were prohibited entry. The head of every family received a piece of agricultural land on which he could work for two days a week to maintain himself and his family; the remainder of the time he worked on the communal fields, which provided produce for the elderly and widows. Hundreds of thousands of cattle and sheep grazed on the pasture lands and provided in abundance for all the households. The Jesuit authorities made sure all were cared for, and organized the education system, labor, the building of houses, church services, and celebrations. No one in the *reducciones* was ever sentenced to death or life imprisonment – something rare in human history.

When the Spanish government extinguished the Jesuits' "holy experiment"[11] as a result of the envy, jealousy, and greed of the colonists, the desperate indigenous residents wrote letters appealing to be allowed to continue their communal way of life. A 1768 letter to Governor Bucareli reads: "We have to tell you that we are not slaves in any way, no more than were our ancestors. We do not like the way in which the Spaniards live without working themselves and without supporting each other."[12]

THE STORIES I HAVE TOLD of these historical utopias are from long ago, and the memory of them has largely been lost. But the questions raised then – as theory in More's *Utopia* and as praxis among the Hutterites and in the Jesuit Missions – still beg for answers, perhaps now more urgently than ever.

At the end of 1933 in Berlin, two strange visitors appeared on the doorstep of Pastor Martin Niemöller, a leader in the Pastors' Emergency League, a network of clergy

Thomas Merton, Dietrich Bonhoeffer, Eberhard Arnold

Photograph of Arnold courtesy of the family. Photograph of Bonhoeffer (public domain). Photograph of Merton by John Lyons.

organized to oppose the Nazification of church life. The two strangers introduced themselves to Niemöller as Hutterites and said that they lived a communistic lifestyle on a Bruderhof, in strict accordance with the Sermon on the Mount. They practiced absolute nonviolence as a basic tenet of their faith.

Niemöller, who had served as a submarine commander in the German imperial navy during World War I, had little sympathy for the two pacifists and ended the conversation quickly. But he reported about the visit to his friend and fellow pastor Dietrich Bonhoeffer, who had recently returned from America. Bonhoeffer was intrigued, and by the summer of 1934 had struck up a relationship with the Bruderhof, meeting with a representative and exchanging letters and manuscripts.[13] Though he planned to visit the Bruderhof community in Germany, this visit never took place; shortly afterward, he assumed leadership of the Confessing Church's illegal theological seminary in Finkenwalde. Here he began his own experiment with Christian community, an experience that would become the basis for his book *Life Together*. In it he described his goals as follows:

Christian brotherhood is not an ideal which we must realize; it is rather a reality created by God in Christ in which we may participate. The more clearly we learn to recognize that the ground and strength and promise of all our fellowship is in Jesus Christ alone, the more serenely shall we think of our fellowship and pray and hope for it.[14]

Bonhoeffer's words could well have been written by the founder of the German Bruderhof, Eberhard Arnold. Born a Lutheran, Arnold had started his Christian fellowship in 1920, partly inspired by the historical Anabaptist communities; in 1930, his community formally joined the Hutterian Church.

Five years after the founding of his community, Arnold set out to explain its new-old way of life in a seminal essay titled "Why We Live in Community."[15] In the 1960s, this essay was discovered by a Trappist monk in North America who was fascinated to discover a kindred spirit in a German Anabaptist who had died three decades earlier. The Trappist's name was Thomas Merton. When Merton, then at the height of his fame, was asked to hold retreats in monasteries in Alaska, he chose to present his lectures in the form of a conversation with Eberhard Arnold. His words, initially addressed to the Catholic religious communities of his day, remain relevant to anyone seeking a way of radical discipleship:

However we look at it, we have this obligation to build community; it isn't just an obligation to one another but to all those who come to us. They need to find true community here, and that is the best thing we can give them.[16]

Is community really the best gift we can give to our fellow human beings? If it is, why don't we get going? Some may object that private ownership is necessary for a happy life because communal life without property inevitably leads to a loss of freedom. But we might equally well ask: Is it possible to achieve genuine peace among humankind as long as claims of ownership and property continue to exist? After all, Francis of Assisi already pointed out eight centuries ago that as long as we have any possessions, we will also require weapons.

The first two decades of the twenty-first century have demonstrated the continuing relevance of these questions, and not only among Christians. Interest in intentional community has revived, and new communitarian movements are emerging. Take for example the network of people inspired by what they call "convivialism," who explain their goals as follows:

> In the face of climate change, financial crises, and mass poverty, a growing number of people agree that we need a fundamental social-ecological transformation that includes all areas of society. Fortunately, a huge variety of concepts and practices for such transformation already exists.[17]

These words point us back to the question with which we started, and which Thomas More raised in his *Utopia*: How then should we live? How do we combine social freedom with equality, solidarity, and justice? How can we achieve a peaceful world in which conflicts are no longer resolved through murderous violence and all people have enough?

These are the questions we must keep asking. ⤵

Translated by Emmy Barth Maendel and Andries Conradie.

1. Gerhard Ritter, translator's note, in Thomas More, *Utopia* (Eberhard Jäckel, 1977), 3–6.3.

2. All quotations from *Utopia* are taken from Henry Morley's translation (Cassel, 1901).

3. Thomas Gehrig, "Commons auf Utopia: Beiträge zur Rückeroberung einer Debatte," in *Express: Zeitung für sozialistische Betriebs- und Gewerkschaftsarbeit,* May 2011.

4. Grete Mecenseffy, *Geschichte des Protestantismus in Österreich* (Graz, 1956).

5. Ibid.

6. Cited in Mecenseffy, *Geschichte des Protestantismus in Österreich.*

7. On the reception history see Terence Cave, *Thomas More's "Utopia" in Early Modern Europe: Paratexts and Contexts* (Manchester University Press, 2008).

8. Christoph Andreas Fischer, *Der Hutterischen Widertauffer Taubenkobel* and *Vier und funfftzig Erhebliche Ursachen, Warumb die Widertauffer nicht sein im Land zu leyden* (Ingolstadt, 1607).

9. Burchard Brentjes, *Atlantis: Geschichte einer Utopie* (DuMont, 1994), 92–95.

10. Ibid.

11. Ibid.

12. Thomas Lange, "Soutanenkaserne oder heiliges Experiment? Die Jesuiten-Reduktionen in Paraguay im europäischen Urteil," in *Mythen der Neuen Welt,* ed. Karl Heinz Kohl (Berlin, 1982), 210–223.

13. Eberhard Arnold, "Bruderhof-Korrespondenz 1934," in *Dietrich-Bonhoeffer-Jahrbuch* 2 (2005/2006), 75–87. For the episode related here see Emmy Barth, *An Embassy Besieged: The Story of a Christian Community in Nazi Germany* (Cascade, 2010).

14. Dietrich Bonhoeffer, *Life Together,* trans. John Doberstein (Harper and Row, 1954), 30.

15. Eberhard Arnold and Thomas Merton, *Why We Live in Community* (Plough, 1995).

16. Ibid., 42.

17. See the website *www.convivialism.org.*

In Search of a City

The church, Scripture teaches, is where God's politics becomes reality: it's a city governed by the Sermon on the Mount. But does any such place exist?

CHARLES E. MOORE

At the outset of my Christian journey, I was taught to keep politics and religion separate. Jesus came to save sinners, not society. Our citizenship is in heaven, not here on earth. It's the soul that counts, not the body. What matters is one's eternal destiny, not social betterment.

This attitude may be appealing to some, but the good news is *good* because it holds promise not only for the next life (which it does) but also for this life and how we live it now. After all, Jesus healed bodies as much as he forgave sins, and he shared everyday life with his followers – eating and drinking and traveling with them – as much as he prayed alone in the wilderness. He announced the arrival of God's politics, which means the end of politics as usual: good news for the poor at the bottom, bad news for the power-elites on top (Luke 6:20–26).

The 2016 presidential campaign made two things painfully clear: Christians do not agree on how to apply the gospel to political issues, and when Christian leaders do get involved in partisan politics, the consequences are hardly benign. Compromise is inevitable, and political intrigue is always close at hand. How, then, to do politics Christianly?

The Activist Temptation

When Ron Sider's seminal book *Rich Christians in a World of Hunger* appeared in 1979, the call for Christian social engagement had an explosive effect on the evangelical world of my youth, which emphasized personal salvation to the exclusion of all else. Today such ideas have become commonplace. Believers from across the theological spectrum seek to end sex trafficking, world hunger, homelessness, environmental depredation, the prison-industrial complex, the death penalty, and a host of other ills. They have marched, petitioned, rallied, advocated, organized, and even peacefully resisted in order to make

Charles E. Moore, a Bruderhof member, teaches at the Mount Academy in New York. He is the editor of a new Plough book, Called to Community: The Life Jesus Wants for His People.

Images © Tubidu Graphics

Brigitta Racz, *Yellow Façade*

society more just and more God-fearing. In the process, they have also discovered firsthand how messy and heartbreaking politics can be.

As a young seminary professor committed to stopping both abortion and poverty, I was not only torn between the competing demands of the right and left but also dismayed by seeing how political power can corrupt even the best of intentions. One day I happened to be in a small gathering of activists who had invited John Howard Yoder to speak. We peppered him with questions: What does it mean to bear witness to Christ's kingdom? What role does the state play in God's economy? What is our political responsibility? What does it mean to bring about social change nonviolently? Yoder listened patiently, then said something I've never forgotten: "The church does not *have* a politic, it *is* a politic."

Yoder's words shocked me into reading the New Testament all over again. And there it was! Jesus wasn't just against violence, injustice, and immorality – he freed people from these very things. He wasn't just against disproportionate and ill-gotten wealth. He was against Mammon itself. He didn't come to sprinkle kingdom values on society. No, his was a society in which God's kingdom broke in (Luke 11:20, 17:21) and where a brand new order emerged (1 Pet. 2:9–12).

Jesus, Yoder taught me, knew full well how this world operated, and that is why he didn't directly confront the Roman state or its policies. He had an entirely different agenda and thus wasn't interested in making Rome, or Israel for that matter, great or even better. These realms were under the grip of principalities and powers that governed by constraint, control, and money. In these kingdoms, you hit back if wronged, and if you had wealth, you secured it for yourself, not for your neighbor. "Not so with you," Jesus told his disciples (Luke 22:24–30). God's kingdom is drastically different (John 18:36). Citizens of his kingdom are inclusive; no one is left out or left behind. They govern themselves by means of the towel, the basin, and the cross. Among his adherents there is neither servant nor lord; all are brothers and sisters who make it their aim to serve the least.

Jesus was more than political; he was radical. By refusing to engage in direct resistance, he bypassed the modus operandi of partisan politics altogether. He rejected means and methods deliberately calculated to manipulate public affairs, even if it was toward some noble end. Instead of using the threat of law, he invited people to pursue the good free-willingly. Jesus offered his followers a new kind of social existence in which the common good took priority. He brought about a new kind of body politic – the body of Christ – in which the good of all and the good of each coalesced into a life of unity and fellowship.

The early chapters of Acts describe such a life. The miracle of Pentecost (Acts 2) was not primarily that people spoke in other tongues but rather that among them natural hierarchies and divisions were overcome. Jesus' first followers shared all things in common and were of one heart, soul, and mind. Their lives were the evidence that the principalities and powers that divide humankind had indeed been defeated on the cross.

The Missing Link

Yoder's words excited me. They also confounded me. Where were the people who forsook politics to live out the justice of God's reign? Countless churches did good works, yet their "social action" seemed to only go so far. Unwed mothers, though directed to crisis pregnancy centers, were later left to fend for themselves. Unemployed Christians still depended more on government assistance than on the church. The elderly were still shunted away in nursing homes, even by those committed to a "focus on the family." The rate of divorce in the church was (and still is) as high as anywhere else. And when it came to conflict or disagreement, power blocks and coercive majorities thrived inside the church just as they did in the secular world. One day the doors of our church were literally chained shut for our failure to comply with new denominational policies regarding women's leadership.

I didn't know where to turn next. If what we read in the New Testament was true, if following Jesus meant adopting a distinct social ethic with others, then something had to give. I wanted to be a part of a community where Jesus was free to be ruler over every sphere of existence. My wife and I made a drastic change and joined the Bruderhof, a communal church or "embassy of the kingdom," where we seek to submit our work, worship, food, housing, and education to the lordship of Christ. Needless to say, it's an imperfect group. Yet here we have found a community of families and singles, highly educated people and high school dropouts, people of all ages and nationalities – all determined to put their faith into practice in unity.

Bruderhof life might look distinctive, but it's not apolitical. It has a body politic all its own. Single mothers and their children, for instance, are not left to fend for themselves; they are connected with other families, receiving the same support as everyone else. The elderly are similarly cherished by family members and other caregivers in the community. They contribute to the community however they can, both practically and spiritually. For example, they

Brigitta Racz, *Morning Shine*

when a collective decision must be made, we strive to wait patiently before God until there is heartfelt unity among all. We promise to address each other directly whenever there is a conflict (which, of course, happens often). If we get stuck, we get help. More important than being in the right is finding joy in one another. We value each other for who we are, as brothers and sisters whose relationships aren't hierarchical but rather make up a fabric where each person is needed and appreciated. Here my wife and I have found a truly different way of living together.

Dropping Out?

This may sound too good to be true. Sometimes, it is – especially when our human missteps lead to situations that are embarrassing, or tragic, or hilarious. And yet, if Jesus is at the center of our common life, we can recognize our failures, look each other in the eye, ask for and grant forgiveness, pick up the pieces, and start fresh. Over and over again. That is doing politics Jesus' way!

While such a life is fulfilling, it is also far from idyllic. It demands a willingness to consciously unmake established patterns of power and advantage. It requires a change of allegiance, one in which our common life and God's cause have priority over our personal wishes.

Does choosing such a life mean dropping out of society and letting the world go to ruin?

spend time with children and teenagers in the community, and younger couples turn to them for parenting advice. In short, they feel needed because they are needed.

When it comes to work, no one is above another – at least, not so long as we're practicing what we preach. All kinds of skills and trainings are valued, and no one receives more because of their position, skill, or expertise. In fact, all of us are paid the same: nothing. We share everything in common, pooling our income so that the love of Jesus can flow unhindered, without envy or possessiveness or financial inequality.

Our pledge is to serve one another in love. So instead of using pressure or manipulation

Brigitta Racz, *Paris, Montmartre*

church can ever seriously be aligned with these forces of injustice and destruction.[1]

A life together with others need not be an escape from the world; it is something we do for the sake of the world. We should always feel responsible for the general welfare of others, but the church serves society best when it embodies the kind of community in which God himself reigns. Only then do we have anything distinctive and life-giving to say.

Ironically, those who in the name of Christ advocate righteous causes by pressuring Congress to pass laws and better spend their tax money usually fail to do justice to the radically communal, and thus political, nature of discipleship. In fact, much of what passes for Christian political activity, on both the left and the right, stems from having despaired of *being* the church. As Hauerwas and Willimon argue in *Resident Aliens,* we fool ourselves whenever we strive through power and partisan politics to make the culture at large a little less racist, a little less promiscuous, a little less violent, a little less unequal and unwelcoming when we ourselves do not practice these things.[2] What we so easily forget is that the church, being the body of Christ, should look like Jesus.

If we make our life in Christ secondary in order to more "effectively" influence society, we are, using an analogy drawn from Yoder, like a musician who leaves the stage in order to work

When Thomas Merton became a Trappist monk, he was criticized for indulging in a way of life that seemed indifferent to the world's problems. His reply was straightforward, even if it was rejected by most:

> By my monastic life and vows I am saying No to all the concentration camps, the aerial bombardments, the staged political trials, the judicial murders, the racial injustices, the economic tyrannies, and the whole socioeconomic apparatus which seems geared for nothing but global destruction in spite of all its fair words in favor of peace. I make monastic silence a protest against the lies of politicians, propagandists, and agitators, and when I speak it is to deny that my faith and my

as an usher in the concert hall.[3] To declare Jesus "Lord" is to say that the essential work of God in history is not within the realm of the old aeon, of power and prestige, but within and between those who make the humble way of the cross central to their lives. Rather than wield power and wealth "as instruments of coercion and pressure, obliging an adversary to yield unconvinced," we should show what life is like when God is on the throne.[4]

The earliest Christians turned the Roman world upside down not because they found ways to better govern society but because they showed what life in the new creation that Christ promised us looks like. Freed of greed, self-interest, power, and pleasures of the flesh, Christians in Rome provided burial for pagans who were too poor to afford it and supported fifteen hundred who were impoverished. In Antioch, the church fed three thousand destitute persons. Church funds, in some cases, bought the emancipation of slaves. When the plague struck Carthage in 252, Bishop Cyprian sent his people out to nurse the sick and bury the dead. A century later, the emperor Julian complained that the Christians looked after "not only their own beggars but ours as well." Their care was so extensive that Julian tried to copy the church's welfare system. In cities filled with homeless people, newcomers, and strangers, and torn by violent ethnic strife, the growing Christian community offered solidarity, help, and hope.[5]

Our society needs people who practice the virtues that make more government unnecessary. It needs people who reimagine and reconfigure their lives so that the reality of God's transforming love can be concretely known and felt. Such a life is political. Such a life is what the New Testament calls the church. It is a matter of doing justice, not just demanding it of others; of building community, not just discussing it; of submitting to one another for the sake of a good greater than oneself, not pushing one's own ideas on others; of sharing with one another so that every need is met, not just one's own. Only in this way can those who suffer under the injustices of this world's system, or from the loneliness and isolation it spawns, have hope of a better way. ⤚

1. Thomas Merton, preface to *The Seven Storey Mountain*, Japanese edition (1966).

2. Stanley Hauerwas and William H. Willimon, *Resident Aliens* (Abingdon, 1989), 80–81.

3. John Howard Yoder, *Discipleship as Political Responsibility* (Herald, 2003), 63.

4. John Howard Yoder, *The Original Revolution* (Herald, 1977), 156.

5. Rodney Stark, *The Rise of Christianity* (HarperSanFrancisco, 1997), 16.

The Church's Task Is to Be the Church

STANLEY HAUERWAS

The first social task of the church is to be the church – the servant community. . . .

Calling for the church to be the church is not a formula for a withdrawal ethic, nor is it a self-righteous attempt to flee from the world's problems. . . . The gospel is political. Christians are engaged in politics, a politics of the kingdom. Such a politics reveals the insufficiency of all politics based on coercion and falsehood, and it finds the true source of power in servanthood rather than domination. . . .

As Christians we are at home in no nation. Our true home is the church itself, where we find those who, like us, have been formed by a savior who was necessarily always on the move.

Source: "The Servant Community: Christian Social Ethics" (1983), in *The Hauerwas Reader*, ed. John Berkman and Michael Cartwright (Duke, 2001), 371–391.

Photographs by Bob Bell

Bob Bell, *Harmony Church Barn*

The Hole in Wendell Berry's Gospel

Why the Agrarian Dream Is Not Enough

TAMARA HILL MURPHY

Wendell Berry, writer, teacher, farmer, and ecological activist, preaches a message America is dying to hear. Doggedly determined to promote an economy built on sustainable agriculture, Berry addresses us in every way he knows how: poems, essays, novels, lectures, and letters. No matter the medium, though, his approach is unrelenting and contrarian. He famously writes books without a computer, farms his Kentucky land without a tractor, and practices his faith without spending much time in church. He is both lauded as a preacher of hope and disparaged as a prophet of doom.

When I read Berry's poems and essays, I sense he and I are kindred spirits. I, too, care about preserving the good, true, and beautiful in a hellbent civilization. On the other hand, when I read Berry's fiction, I begin to suspect he would not much approve of me. I read as if I were an adolescent who is constantly objecting "Yeah, but . . ." to the author's often narrow view of the good life and his criticisms of anyone who wanders off the path. I can be contrarian, too, Mr. Berry.

I read about the Coulters and the Proudfoots and the Branches and perhaps his most beloved protagonist, Jayber Crow, as if I know them personally, and often I find they don't represent themselves altogether truthfully. Maybe I feel close to them because two generations back both sides of my family lived in Port William–type villages in the center of New York State. When Mr. Crow moves to his final home on a riverbank, I feel like he's speaking my family dialect. I know exactly the "substantial sound" of an anchor line plunking into the bottom of a boat, and the language of a single fish slurping from the surface of a still pond. I know it because, by the grace of God and kindly grandparents, I've spent countless childhood days on a quiet waterfront. But also, I know it because it's embedded in my genes from my grandfather's generation, who lived in a small village dotted with pastures and bubbling brooks.

The dissonance with Berry occurs when I consider other family tales buried under the agrarian beauty. These are stories of shattered relationships, addiction, job loss, abandonment, mental illness, and unspoken violations that seem to separate my kinfolk from the clans in Port William. In Berry's fictional village, readers occasionally witness felonies, infidelity, drunken brawls, and tragic deaths, but all of them seem to be told in a dusky, warming light.

The pleasure I experience reading a novel set in idyllic Port William, before war, agribusiness, and corporate industrialism pillage the town, turns quickly from a nostalgic glow to an ugly flame. I agree with the author's animosity toward institutional and human greed, but I'm troubled by the apparent evils he chooses to overlook. Berry seems to cast mercy on certain kinds of frailties and judgment on others. As a loyal reader, this double standard agitates me: I become a mad reader of the Mad Farmer.

Berry's body of work lauds an unadulterated ecosphere. How does he reconcile glossing over (or at least hiding from his reader's view) the ugly dysfunctions that often prosper alongside the natural beauty of such villages and pasturelands? The stories I grew up hearing and observing provide an alternative cast of characters to the Port William community. I've seen firsthand not only the ornery nature of such characters but also the ingrown thinking that sometimes flourishes in out-of-sight locales. For example, there's the good country farmer I watched with my own eyes fist-beat his son. They seemed to keep their farm by the mad farmer's standards, but that did not make them good. I tiptoe around extended family members who fought their whole lives like Jayber Crow to avoid answering to "the man across the desk," yet leave a trail of fractured relationships in their wake.

My grandmother's father – a Port Williamesque man – abandoned my grandmother when she was eight because his new wife didn't like her or her older sister. Their country village, apparently, did not reject him for his decision – going so far as to make him an elected official. They likely tended their own gardens, gathered their own eggs, and milked their own cows. Their love for land and place did not require a father to love his own daughter. The authenticity of their economics did not guarantee a purity of heart.

In the recently released memoir *Hillbilly Elegy: A Family and Culture in Crisis*, author J. D. Vance shares his experience of growing up in a white, working-poor community in rural

> **The dissonance with Berry occurs when I consider other family tales buried under the agrarian beauty.**

Tamara Hill Murphy, a freelance writer, lives with her husband Brian in Fairfield, Connecticut.

Kentucky. His story picks up where Berry's usually leaves off – just after the rural folk give up their farms and move to the city for other employment. The theme of loss mirrors the lament Berry sounds in his entire body of work: loss of land, loss of livelihood, and loss of a richly storied culture. There's also the loss of thousands of residents who leave for the promise of manufacturing jobs elsewhere. For Vance's family, that elsewhere was a Rust Belt town in neighboring Ohio. Berry's fiction and Vance's memoir diverge at the point of community and family relationships, and the real-world stories are not charming in the least. Drunken brawls in one generation become opiate-induced felonies in the next, all resulting in childhood memories of shattering abuse and aching neglect.

There is no hazy glow concealing the conspicuous demons in Vance's community. Where Berry seems to place blame on external forces, Vance is all too aware of how families pass down dysfunction, no matter what state the economy is in. Because Berry has a meticulous understanding of symbiotic ecological systems, I feel like no one should understand this truth better. How can Berry see so clearly the connection between man and nature, dependent on each other, and yet appear willing to overlook the interdependence of generations?

Instead, Port Williams' characters serve as a mouthpiece for an author bemoaning every generation to come along since the Depression who dared to purchase produce from a supermarket or drive their car across the river to see what was on the other side. I mourn the same losses, and still, if I could speak to Jayber Crow (a.k.a. Wendell Berry) I'd have to ask, "What about the sins of the fathers?" Since we share the same theology of free will and depravity of man, I know not to make them

solely responsible. Neither should Berry make them entirely (romantically) blameless.

The adage "ideals blind us" might be a good caution as we engage with economic manifestos – fictional or otherwise. Would Berry's writing be more truthful if he applied his love of place to the subsequent generations of those displaced from it? In story terms: What happens to Maddie Keith's children and Hannah Coulter's great-grandchildren? In real-world terms: How can the disenfranchised working class of Vance's generation – and of the rest of this hellbent-on-upward-mobility civilization – be redeemed? How, in the words of Wendell Berry, can we "practice resurrection" now?

Berry and Vance both include some important trail markers from their grandparents' generation. In his 2012 Jefferson Lecture in the Humanities, Berry tells the story of his grandfather – a simple tobacco farmer in rural Kentucky – who devoted his life to repairing soil he had exposed to erosion in a misguided attempt to "plow his way out of debt." Berry sees this as one of the most honorable things he remembers about his grandfather, and I would agree. Similarly, in Vance's memoir, he recalls one of his grandfather's rare acts of remorse. After bailing out his drug-addicted daughter (Vance's mother) yet one more time, "Papaw buried his head in his hands and did something Uncle Jimmy had never seen him do: He wept. 'I've failed her; I've failed my baby girl.'" Vance transforms this story into an opportunity for generational reflection:

> Papaw's rare breakdown strikes at the heart of an important question for hillbillies like me: How much of our lives, good and bad, should we credit to our personal decisions, and how much is just the inheritance of our culture, our families, and our parents who have failed their children?

Bob Bell, *Kentucky Barn*

Both grandfathers display the sort of response – dare I say, repentance – lacking in Berry's Port William. The result can be that we, the readers, long for a dishonest ideal. Rather than a wistful reading of Berry's fictionalized world as too good to be true, I would propose that Port William – even before the plunder of corporate industrialism – is not good enough. If Port William signifies the American Dream, then it is good only to the extent that its self-described "membership" is expansive enough to welcome the displaced and uninitiated. It is honorable to the extent that it righteously protests every sort of threat to both human and natural environments.

This dream is too large to be contained at a local or even national level; it requires a gospel-sized imagination. Through this lens, we can imagine the sort of grace that roots us with affection for the place we live, yes, but over-flows the bounds of time and place with the ever-sustained economy of Christ's kingdom.

In my life and in the family stories handed down to me, I've learned the cost of misaligned devotion to an ideal. No one has spoken more

clearly to me on the subject than Dietrich Bonhoeffer, the German theologian, in his *Life Together*:

> In Christian brotherhood everything depends upon its being clear right from the beginning . . . that Christian brotherhood is not an ideal, but a divine reality. . . . Just as surely as God desires to lead us to a knowledge of genuine Christian fellowship, so surely must we be overwhelmed by a great disillusionment with others, with Christians in general, and, if we are fortunate, with ourselves. . . . A community which cannot bear and cannot survive such a crisis, which insists upon keeping its illusion when it should be shattered, permanently loses in that moment the promise of Christian community. Sooner or later it will collapse.

Those of us who live within the divine reality Bonhoeffer describes can ask this question with even more clarity: In what ways might our allegiance to ideals (agrarian or otherwise) diverge from the gospel reality? In Port William, Berry envisions membership in a special kind of community, bound by mutual affection for a way of life; in the teachings of Christ we are given a vision for an even larger community, a kingdom where mercy and judgment meet in his life, death, resurrection, and ascension. A gospel-sized economic model is not about sustaining an ideal, but about redeeming one.

My small-town lineage tells its own redemption stories. Now that I've grown more humble in years, I can better see the broken web of redemption in them. Every time my paternal grandfather plays the banjo for dancing great-grandchildren, he mirrors the good of his own father, a legendary jolly singer of tunes (even if he'd been drinking). My maternal grandmother, left on the doorstep of a stranger, with only one tiny suitcase the size of my laptop to hold all her belongings, once told a circle of her daughters and grandchildren it was the best thing that ever happened to her: "That was the house where I met Jesus, right on the knee of my foster mother."

> **A Gospel-sized economic model is not about sustaining an ideal, but about redeeming one.**

Her stories of that home and that life mixed tragedy and humor – milking cows, emptying chamber pots for wealthy Catskill tourists, waving goodbye to her foster father as he left for his daily milk truck delivery. One of those mornings, his truck collided with a train, leaving my grandmother fatherless again. My grandmother and her foster mother took in boarders to make a living. A living that I'm quite certain Berry would approve of.

In her own way, I think my grandmother's life offers a profound response to the tension between generational interdependence and personal responsibility. A few weeks ago, I discovered her diary from 1931, the year she graduated from high school. In each entry, I could see the way her life was shaped around the woman who took her in as a daughter, and I was thankful all over again for that salvation. Reading between the lines, I could also hear the voice of a lonely teenage girl trying to do good and be good with a sort of forced cheerfulness. Still today, her children, grandchildren, and great-grandchildren are trying to make sense of this sort of heartache.

A discerning reader will notice similar moments of real-world redemption woven into Berry's novels. Jayber Crow, the beloved barber of Port William, tries to sort out the complex web of redemption at the end of his life. His reflection sounds a bit like a gospel-scaled economy:

> This is, as I said and believe, a book about Heaven, but I must say too that it has been a close call. For I have wondered sometimes if it would not finally turn out to be a book about Hell – where we fail to love one another, where we hate and destroy one another for reasons abundantly provided or for righteousness' sake or for pleasure, where we destroy the things we need the most, where we see no hope and have no faith, where we are needy and alone, where things that ought to stay together fall apart, where there is such a groaning travail of selfishness in all its forms, where we love one another and die, where we must lose everything to know what we have had.

Those of us who wish to emulate his ideals will receive the greatest gift from Berry's words by reading through a gospel – rather than an idealistic – lens, because the gospel of Christ is the only economy sturdy enough to save us all. ➷

Photographs courtesy of John Noltner

American Stories

JOHN NOLTNER

Frustrated with the world's focus on what separates us, I set out to use my photography and journalism to explore the common humanity that connects us. Over three years, I drove forty thousand miles across the United States, asking people, "What does peace mean to you?"

It's a simple question, but one that quickly gets to the core of who we are as human beings and what we value as a society. It opens the door to conversations about our greatest hopes and deepest fears. It leads to dialog about race, gender, faith, justice, conflict resolution, civic responsibility, and social change.

In each case, we sat down for an hour-long recorded interview, and then I took the person's portrait. The results are shared in a book, *A Peace of My Mind: American Stories*, in a podcast, and in a traveling exhibit. I interviewed people from many backgrounds and walks of life, but in the following pages I'd like to introduce you to a few of the first-generation immigrants I met, who have each made this nation of immigrants a better place.

Certainly there are problems in the world that could put us at odds and turn us into enemies. But what if we shifted that focus? What if we emphasized the beauty and good in one another? What if we celebrated examples of positive change? What if we simply took the time to listen to one another? ▪

Above, César, an undocumented Mexican immigrant, crossed the border on foot at age sixteen.

John Noltner, a Minnesota-based freelance photographer for national magazines and Fortune 500 companies, founded A Peace of My Mind in 2009. Visit apomm.net *to learn more.*

Talat Hamdani immigrated to the United States from Pakistan in 1979. On September 11, 2001, her son Salman, an NYPD cadet and an EMT, didn't come home. Talat searched the hospitals and morgues, but found no trace of her son. Because of his Muslim faith, some surmised that he was complicit in the terror attacks. Six months later, Salman's remains were found at Ground Zero with an EMT bag by his side. He had given his life trying to save others.

> "How is our pain different? How is your pain superior to my pain?"

In fourth grade, Salman came home from Catholic school and said, "I don't want to go to school anymore, Mama. Other kids say, 'You're not a Catholic. Why are you coming here?'"

I went to the principal and she said, "Don't worry, I'll take care of it." A couple of days later he came home and said, "I need a copy of the Qu'ran to bring to school. Our social studies teacher told the whole class to bring in their book of faith." That is what this country needs: education about other faiths and tolerance and diversity.

My objective is to show the American people – especially non-Muslims – the face of a Muslim who died that day, show them that his family suffers the same pain as anyone else. Just because we are of a different faith doesn't mean that the pain is less, or that we don't miss our child, or that we are insensitive or cruel. No, you cut, we bleed. ∎

Yanina Calderone was born in Guatemala City. She moved to New York City at age fourteen to live with her father. Yanina was raped at age fifteen and became pregnant. She decided to keep her child. Rather than let a violent act ruin her life, she chose to funnel all of her love toward her child. When Yanina left an abusive husband, she made ends meet by selling drugs, got addicted to heroin, and joined a street gang. Today she participates in Alternatives to Violence Project, a program that teaches nonviolent conflict resolution.

> "I let go all of the hurt and decided to do something for others instead of me."

There was this lady who was going through domestic violence. I knew it, but I didn't ever say anything until that day I saw her crying. I talked to her. I said, "Are you afraid of him? Don't be. That's how they get you." She asked for help.

I'm like, "I helped somebody. I can do this more often." I have so many experiences in my life: addict, victim of domestic violence, rape victim. I can talk about it now. For seventeen, eighteen years, I never told nobody that I was raped. I never told no one that I had a son from rape.

I don't regret what I have done in life because it allows me to help others. If I can stop you, I stop you. ■

Penina Bowman was seventeen years old when soldiers showed up at her home in Hungary and told her family they had twenty minutes to pack their bags. They were told they were being sent away to work, but the train brought them to Auschwitz. Penina lost her parents and forty-two other relatives to the Holocaust, but she and her siblings survived.

"I don't hate anybody. Hate is a very powerful thing. It destroys you instead of other people."

My two sisters and I stuck together and that's what helped us survive. When one of us was down, we would encourage each other. We prayed. Psychologically, I think prayer helps. I didn't lose my faith and I didn't lose my sanity. Having something to believe in helped us survive.

When I first came to the United States, I saw so many of my fellow Holocaust survivors who were destroying themselves because of their hate. They couldn't enjoy life, they couldn't go on with their lives, and I said, "This is not going to happen to me."

I would not wish war on anybody. People don't realize what it means to live with guns and soldiers and the fear that you're going to be killed any minute. And the worst part is that people don't appreciate what they have. Because of what I went through, I learned to appreciate everything and not make a big deal out of little things. I let them be. ∎

Chris Okere Odundo grew up in Kibera, one of the largest slums in the world, outside of Nairobi, Kenya. Seeing a lack of fundamental sanitation, Chris started a nonprofit organization called Power of Hope Kibera to address basic health and hygiene issues. He met his wife when she visited the slum working on similar issues for a US-based nonprofit. They now run Power of Hope Kibera together out of Boulder, Colorado.

"If you want to make peace in a place it takes time."

I can say that in Kibera people love each other and there is peace and joy. What sometimes does take away my peace is people who stay here in America and think there is no hope for them. They don't come and talk to the people.

I try to bring youth together because they say that youth can do anything to make peace happen or not happen in a place – they are very flexible to do anything. I try to come up with meetings and talk to them: "We need to come together, love each other, and work together so that we have peace, because if we have peace we will go far." Sometimes they listen and sometimes they don't.

In Kibera you find dogs barking everywhere. If you try to stop the dogs barking, you can't reach your destination. So I'll leave alone the dogs that are barking without any benefit and go forward, and I'll make it to my destination instead of focusing on the dogs that are just making noise. ■

Julissa Arce came to the United States when she was eleven and became undocumented three years later when her visa expired. She paid for college by operating a funnel cake stand and graduated with a degree in finance. Using false papers, she landed an internship at Goldman Sachs, was offered a full-time job, and eventually became a vice president. Today she is an American citizen and an advocate for immigration reform.

"We should be thinking of the eleven million people affected by the inaction of our country."

If my English isn't very good and I'm working as a waitress or a dishwasher at a restaurant, people are going to question me. But because I was working at Goldman Sachs and graduated cum laude from a top business school, no one was ever going to think twice about me or question my credentials.

It's easy to place the blame on a group of people who don't have a voice, who don't have representation. That's what is happening. How is it possible that we can blame eleven million people [undocumented immigrants] for all of our problems?

Eleven million people currently cannot live as full human beings. Eleven million people are scared every day of being separated from their families. If they're driving down the street and get pulled over, they will be deported. I know what it's like to live with that fear. That should be at the center of the conversation, because it's a human rights issue. ∎

Hassan Ikhzaan Saleem was born in the Maldives. Raised in a family that encouraged reading western classic literature, he fell in love with the American West and the idea of working with horses. He attended college in New Mexico and lived with a family that owned a ranch. There he learned to ride horses and to train them in the Vaquero style, with a focus on patience.

I work with this red horse, Caspian. We work and we get

things done and I'm so proud of myself. I come back next morning and he's forgotten everything or I've forgotten everything, and it doesn't work. It's hard to be calm at that moment. I get frustrated. I get mad. But tomorrow is a new day. All is forgiven.

I'm not Mahatma Gandhi. I'm not Martin Luther King Jr. or Nelson Mandela. My parents said to me, "You might never change the world and you might never see the change you want to see, but at least you tried." So that's why I try. Even with horses. People say, "Aw, you've been working with this horse for six months, he still sucks." And I say, "Well, I'll keep trying, and one day that horse will be great and I'll ride him in the biggest rodeo. I'm going to take him up in the high country and pull a steer, and it'll be the most beautiful thing in the world." ■ ⤳

"If humans were like horses, there'd be more peace on earth."

I Am My Enemy

A naturalized American finds herself at war with her homeland.

LUMA SIMMS

The Lion of Babylon, a widely recognized symbol of Iraqi culture, is a figure on the Ishtar Gate, built by Nebuchadnezzar in 575 BC.

Luma Puma – that's what the American kids called me. Luma Puma Montezuma. Their ridicule made me wish I had never come to America. It made me hate my name and where I was from. It made me hate everything about myself.

I was born in Baghdad, to a Chaldean Catholic mother and a Syriac Orthodox father, but all my ancestors were born in Mosul and neighboring cities in northern Iraq. For many years, no matter where I was living, I would answer the question "Where are you from?" with "I am from Mosul." Such is the existential reality of first-generation immigrants: the both/and tension of two civilizations within oneself, the wistful desire for one identity, one culture, one homeland, one whole and integral worldview.

My early years in Iraq are full of vivid memories: I remember dipping my *khubiz* (pita bread) in the *chi u halib* (tea and milk) my grandmother used to make for me, and my uncle taking me out for *zlabya*, a syrup-drenched fried dough. I remember belly-dancing to the claps and hurrahs of my grandparents. My father taught entomology, botany, and beekeeping. My mother taught at a high school.

But our life in Iraq was not idyllic. My father was played as a pawn and a scapegoat between the Shiites and Sunnis at work. My mother was forced to adopt Muslim dress in the market.

Luma Simms is an associate fellow at The Philos Project and the author of Gospel Amnesia: Forgetting the Goodness of the News.

Image from www.ancient.eu/Ishtar_Gate

Image from Wikimedia Commons (public domain)

I sometimes came home from school crying because my teacher hit my palms with a ruler. The Muslim teachers were always harder on the Christian students – at least that's how it seemed to those of us in the Christian community. I'll never forget the day my mother came home angry that I was ranked second in my class while first place was given to a Muslim girl who scored a point higher in only one subject – physical education. It wasn't long after that episode that I started hearing my parents talk about how we had "no future in this country." By the time I started coming home from school singing Ba'ath party propaganda songs, they had made up their minds.

Leaving Iraq

My dad sold his Fiat, and we packed our suitcases and said we were going on vacation to Greece. Once we arrived in Athens, my father began the long process of seeking asylum. After applying to many countries for permanent immigration and getting turned down, we heard that an Armenian family in Los Angeles had offered to sponsor us. I didn't want to move again; I wanted to stay in Greece or go back to Iraq. I missed my grandparents. My mom tried to cheer me up by promising to buy bananas and oranges for me when we arrived in our new home.

Our plane touched down in Los Angeles on December 13, 1978. The shock of migrating from an Eastern civilization and worldview to the West was like a collision in my very being. We settled in Fullerton, California, where there were no Iraqis or Arabs at the time, at least none we knew of. Every weekend, we would make the thirty-mile drive to Los Angeles to visit the only other Iraqis we knew, the Armenian family who had sponsored us. Between weekends, however, it was hard to communicate with my classmates, teachers, and other members of our community. I knew four English words: yes, no, please, and thank you.

The first month we were in America, we went to an evangelical church in Fullerton. My parents left me in Sunday school; that's what was supposed to be done, they were told. When snack time came, I was given a banana and two pieces of brown bread with brown filling inside. I had never tasted peanut butter before, but I was starving. I bit into the sandwich and my mouth filled with the dry, sticky stuff. My lips felt like they'd been glued together. I wanted

A US soldier frisks an elderly Iraqi during the 1991 invasion.

Photograph © Johnny Saunderson / Alamy Stock Photo

to cry, but I was afraid the other kids would make fun of me. Holding back tears, I walked to the front of the classroom and held out the peanut butter sandwich with one hand and the banana with the other. I was trying to ask the teacher for permission *not* to eat the sandwich. I motioned with both hands, trying to ask if I could have the banana without the sandwich. The teacher thought I wanted the sandwich but not the banana. So she took the banana and left me with the peanut butter sandwich. I went and sat down, tears streaming down my face.

The internal turmoil of those years has never left me. It has shaped me and informed how I view human identity and immigration.

Soon after arriving in California, my parents found jobs. With no close relatives or family friends nearby to watch us, my sister and I became latchkey kids. During the summers, the library was our nanny. In the fourth grade at Raymond Elementary School, I struggled to understand the teacher and my peers. One scene is burned into my memory – the teacher sitting in the front of the classroom on a stool and reading from a book. For a few moments, time stood still and my soul rested from its turmoil. I didn't understand a word that was read, but I memorized the picture on the front; it was *Charlotte's Web*. I devoured it as soon as I could read English for myself. Reading saved my life; it continues to do so.

My Country My Enemy?

When the Iran hostage crisis happened, my father lamented that the problems of the Middle East had followed us to America. My parents warned us not to say we were from Iraq, lest people would think we supported what was happening, which we obviously did not. "Just say you're from Greece if anyone asks," they told us. When the eight-year Iran-Iraq War broke out in 1980, my parents were relieved that we lived in America. My father had been spared from being drafted into the army. Another family member, however, was sent to the front lines. Phone calls for updates were brief and carefully worded – you never knew who was listening, and everyone in the country lived in fear of Saddam Hussein's government. We heard reports of schoolchildren tricked into informing on their parents, and anyone who spoke out against Saddam could be imprisoned or killed.

In 1990, Saddam invaded Kuwait. And then came January 16, 1991, the day my naturalized country, America, invaded the country of my birth and heritage, Iraq. It was the most dissonant moment of my life. I wept. I prayed that my beloved family members would survive. I felt my dual identity being tested. Once again, my family became fearful that others would judge us if they knew we were Iraqis. We tried to avoid saying where we were from when in mixed company. Yet, even among other people from our homeland, we weren't free from conflict. Every time we gathered with other Iraqi friends, arguments would break out: "It's Saddam's fault, he deserves it!" "No, it was the Americans who made him their pawn in the region, and now they have turned on him." On and on it went, but it was just talk – none of us could do anything about any of it.

There was a time when Iraq was an up-and-coming country. It had well-paved roads and modern buildings, plumbing, and other infrastructure and institutions. Watching Arabic movies from the 1960s, the average American would see a recognizably modern society. Family life flourished, women were educated, and the household-based culture thrived, in spite of new philosophies from the West trickling in through those who had studied abroad. The relationship between Christians and Muslims may not have been ideal, but there was no bloodshed. The country has now been set back decades, some might say centuries. The buildings are worn, peeling, and broken. There is uncertainty and doubt about the rebuilding of the old structures, whether material or social.

What makes my heart ache even more than the material damage is a particular marker of the disintegration of family life. Where once there was *not one* nursing home in all of Baghdad (families always took care of their elderly), currently there are at least two, in part because so many young Iraqis have fled the country. This is not merely a matter of a demographic shift; it's a symptom of a change in mindset that now allows the younger generation to abandon their elders.

The land of my ancestors, the land where I was born and where I lived for the first seven years of my life, has been utterly destroyed by wave after wave of violence. Iraq's people are fatigued, demoralized, and in cultural and economic distress. Even if we are able to drive ISIS out of Iraq, we must encourage our government to think beyond a military outcome. And since America had a hand in bringing about this turn of events, it bears a great responsibility for the work of healing and rebuilding the country.

Belonging and Not Belonging

Abraham, my ancestor, was living in Ur, in Mesopotamia, when God called him out of the land of his fathers to be a pilgrim and a sojourner until the day when God would give him and his descendants the land of Canaan (now the land of Israel). In the New Testament the life of a Christian is described as a pilgrimage to a new country, our heavenly home. I don't know how Abraham did it, but I've always felt very acutely that I didn't belong.

Perhaps this is why, in recent years, I have not been surprised to see the rise of nationalist movements in the West. Though the details may differ, they are all variations on the same theme: a civilizational crisis rooted in an identity crisis. The West has, to a great extent, rejected its cultural and spiritual patrimony, which was rooted in biblical values. Pair this phenomenon with an influx of immigrants – especially from the Middle East – who for one reason or another are not assimilating to Western political, philosophical, and cultural thought. We don't need to be political philosophers to understand what we are seeing as we watch one civilization struggling against another. We feel it existentially.

Many of us have begun asking: "Who am I, and who are we as a nation?" These questions of identity lead to questions of nationality. And no one feels this dissonance more deeply than immigrants. An immigrant, particularly one who has crossed a civilizational boundary in addition to a national border, will almost invariably undergo an identity crisis. This is why understanding the mindset of immigrants

> We must stop trying to style peoples and countries in our image. We are not their Creator.

is crucial to understanding the crisis many in the world are undergoing.

The most salient fact for Americans and the American government to grasp about Iraq (or any non-Western country) is that there is a non-Western paradigm and worldview, and it is valid. There is another way of living, building an economy, and governing than what we know in the West. Certainly I am not equating paved roads and plumbing with cultural imperialism; I am referring to relationships, political negotiations, and how people value their own sense of well-being. You can debate Iraq's merits all you want, but respect the people, their land, their culture, and their way of life. Iraq will never become America, and we must stop trying to style peoples and countries in our image. We are not their Creator. If we are to play a role in rebuilding the nation, we must do so in their interest, not ours. Bringing freedom to a people starts with respecting them as a people in their own right. This may seem a small matter, but it is imperative to understand. Out of this mentality will flow a different rebuilding and healing strategy.

Where East and West Meet

These days, when people find out I am an Iraqi Christian, they ask how I feel or what I think about what's happening in the Middle East. My emotions and thoughts are complex. In the case of ISIS in Iraq, the culture being destroyed is my heritage, the people being killed are my kin. I am told to love my enemy, but what does loving your enemy mean when he's holding a gun to your head or a sword to your neck? The immigrant mind is complex, and in this age of a major refugee crisis and vast movements of people, working toward a shared understanding is vital.

My mom used to say: "If you deny your origin, you deny yourself." I have lived long enough to know this to be true. No matter where I am in the world, however, I take comfort in knowing I am always part of the kingdom of God. In the Old Testament book of Jeremiah, the prophet writes a letter to the exiles in Babylon:

> Thus says the Lord of hosts, the God of Israel, to all the exiles whom I have sent into exile from Jerusalem to Babylon: Build houses and live in them; plant gardens and eat what they produce. Take wives and have sons and daughters; takes wives for your sons, and give your daughters in marriage, that they may bear sons and daughters; multiply there, and do not decrease. But seek the welfare of the city where I have sent you into exile, and pray to the Lord on its behalf, for in its welfare you will find your welfare. (Jer. 29:4–7)

As internally disordered as I've felt at different times in my life, with the American me in conflict with the Iraqi me, my Christian faith has always brought sense to my life as an immigrant – and solace, to some degree. Through the prophet Isaiah, God says this:

> Do not fear, for I am with you; I will bring your offspring from the east, and from the west I will gather you; I will say to the north, "Give them up," and to the south, "Do not withhold; bring my sons from far away and my daughters from the end of the earth – everyone who is called by my name, whom I created for my glory, whom I formed and made." (Isa. 43:5–7)

I am a daughter whom he brought from the East. It was in the West that he recreated me into who he wanted me to become – a synthesis of East and West – and gathered me into his kingdom, where all his people become one. ⤳

Image from www.opendoorsusa.org

EDDIE LYLE

The Real Radicals

Face to Face with the Persecuted Church

Devout, determined, and deadly, the young man was prepared to wage jihad. But only a few hours before he planned to take action, everything changed. He had a vision of Christ. Right then, the jihadi gave his life to Jesus.

Fearing for his life, he was forced to flee his home and is now living under a new identity in a different country. I met this remarkable brother through my work with Open Doors, an organization serving persecuted Christians worldwide. As I've learned in the course of my work, his story is far from unique.

More and more people from Muslim backgrounds are turning to Christ – and risking their lives to do so. For example, about forty years ago, some two hundred Christians from Muslim backgrounds were living in Iran; today that estimate is 370,000, though precise numbers are hard to come by.

So how are these conversions happening? Often, it seems, Jesus is meeting Muslims and occasionally even jihadis in dreams. One former jihadi spoke of a dream in which he was pulled from a fast-moving river by a man

---

Eddie Lyle is president of Open Doors UK & Ireland.

Christian women gather at a church in Erbil, Iraq, to mourn the death of a member of their community (August 2016).

Photograph by Alice Martins/AP Photo

dressed in white. Another convert had two visions of Jesus, in which he was instructed to go to a certain location where a pastor would give him a Bible. He obeyed, and even though he'd never met the pastor before, the pastor was expecting him and even knew his name.

Some stories we hear mirror those of the Bible. Amir (not his real name), a well-respected haji, having made the pilgrimage to Mecca, could be seen as a modern-day Paul. When Amir's daughter converted to Christianity, he was angry, and when his wife and later his son also came to Christ, he began to persecute them. He beat them and forbade them to visit the church, saying he would inform the secret police, and even threatened to kill them. But his family did not leave Christ – they left him by fleeing abroad.

In his loneliness, Amir focused on Allah, begging for revelation. But the subsequent silence made him doubt. Had his family been right? He didn't know whether to believe in Allah or Jesus, the Bible or the Qu'ran. Finally he said, "I will believe in the God who reveals himself to me."

Amir's prayers were answered in a dream in which a man approached him riding a donkey. He had never seen the man before, but the man hugged him and said, "I will cleanse you of all your sins; you are free. I will give you rest. Believe in me." When the man departed, another approached and told Amir that the man on the donkey was Jesus Christ.

The next night, Amir had the same dream. When he woke, he felt afraid. He'd served Allah for forty-five years and had made the haj. How could he leave Islam? But the following night, he had the same dream for the third time. Amir knew he had found God, but he did not know what to do next. Even though he'd forbidden his family to go to the local church, he knew he'd learn more about the man on the donkey there and decided to attend.

At first, the congregants were suspicious. Wasn't this the man who had threatened to kill his family because they accepted Christ? But when he told them he had met Christ in a dream and wanted to give his life to Jesus, the church leaders began to trust him. Soon Amir was involved in ministry, risking his life for his faith. When his family abroad heard what had happened, they praised God for answering their prayers and happily accepted Amir back into the family. Since leaving his country and reuniting with them, Amir enjoys the novel experience of going to church without fear.

Baptism Means Danger

Conversions like Amir's do not come without cost. Many converts from Islam face discrimination and exclusion. Some suffer beatings, and others have paid the ultimate price for their faith in Christ. However, even the threat of violence doesn't stop converts from Islam from wanting to be baptized. A baptism, usually a very public declaration of a private commitment to faith, must be conducted in secret so as not to endanger the local Christian community.

At Open Doors, we support our persecuted brothers and sisters and share the gospel where it is forbidden. Our annual World Watch List identifies the top fifty countries in which it is most difficult to be a Christian. In 2016, eight of the top ten countries cited Islamic extremism as the primary reason for persecution, and thirty-five out of the top fifty reported as much.

In this context, we're called not only to pray for conversions from Islam but to nurture new believers. Studies have shown that in parts of the Middle East, many Muslim-background believers return to Islam if they do not receive support within six months of coming to faith. Thus, it's imperative to reach new believers quickly to support them in the isolation and danger they experience. A sustaining Christian community is vital for people who may have lost their status, family, and livelihood because of their commitment to Christ. New believers must also have access to the Scriptures. This is why smuggling Bibles is as important to Open Doors today as it was to our founder, Brother Andrew, in the 1950s.

Smuggling Hope

In 1957, Andrew van der Bijl loaded up the back of his battered Volkswagen Beetle with Bibles and Christian literature. He drove to Moscow, directly violating the laws of the Soviet Union, which forbade religious literature. He

prayed as he passed through checkpoints and miraculously succeeded in meeting Christians and handing out the Bibles. When people asked him his name, he said, "I am a brother to all those who love and follow Jesus Christ." Through these journeys, he became known as Brother Andrew.

Just as Brother Andrew did decades ago, we're still smuggling Bibles and Christian literature into closed countries – often at great personal risk. Of course, in the digital age we have more opportunities than ever to get the Word of God to the people most hungry for it. Of the 355 million people living in the Middle East, about 50 percent now have access to the internet. Open Doors' social media projects focus on supporting Christians in the Arabic-speaking world. This includes helping parents teach their children the values of the kingdom of God as they grow up. For example, for parents from cultures where boys are valued more than girls, it is important to share stories of a God who values everyone equally.

Tens of thousands of people from all over the Middle East, from Morocco and Libya to the Arabian Peninsula, take part in Open Doors' online community. But the goal is to get people engaged not only online but also in a local church. To this end, an online support team operating from inside the region is available to minister to people in contact with us.

Online connections can have an offline impact. According to one local coordinator, a frequent visitor from Iraq "likes to visit our page because she feels [it] makes a difference in her life and plays an important role in her

Brother Andrew and his Volkswagen Beetle, which he filled with Bibles to smuggle into the Soviet Union in 1957.

Open Doors' Arabic Bible app, showing 1 Thessalonians 2

Image from Wikimedia Commons (public domain)

spiritual growth. . . . She shares the posts, stories, and subjects . . . to stimulate discussions with her friends. She notices a big difference in her friends' lives in the midst of all the difficulties they are facing in Iraq right now."

Other visitors struggle with loneliness and begin seeking God after having been touched by one of the uplifting stories posted online. A regional coordinator describes connecting with a young man from the Arabian Peninsula: "He contacted us, and now we are speaking with him about his relationship with the Lord. We are encouraging him to keep praying and reading the Bible. He said that he feels safe with us and that we've helped him grow spiritually and overcome his loneliness."

Through social media, Open Doors is able to connect directly with Christians in closed countries where churches are struggling to give a public witness. Interestingly, Muslims who may be open to Christ are also seemingly at ease communicating anonymously online. One Muslim woman expressed her appreciation for our Facebook page and for the deep questions it raises. She said that many people in her country have questions about difficult religious issues. We suggested she begin reading the Bible and sent her a link to a clip that explains its message. Since then, she has begun to share her questions about the Bible, and we've continued our conversation with her.

As free encrypted messaging services such as WhatsApp continue to grow, so will our opportunities to minister to people's needs. This is why, in part, Open Doors has launched a seven-year global campaign called Hope for the Middle East. The church in the West dare not stand by while extremism threatens the very existence of the church in the Middle East.

A few years ago, in an Islamic country where Christians are persecuted, Brother Andrew baptized twelve men who had converted from Islam. Because of the need for discretion, Brother Andrew used a shallow inflatable swimming pool for the occasion. Some of them insisted they wanted to go "all the way under." As one elderly man who'd suffered a stroke six months earlier emerged from the water, he waved his right hand. The stroke had paralyzed his right side; yet in his baptism he was completely healed. Two years later, this man was martyred by extremists because he would not stop teaching the Bible and testifying about how Jesus had changed his life.

Such experiences of God's work in closed countries lead me to believe that no threat, no law, and no terror can stifle the Holy Spirit. We must continue to pray, share, speak out, and place ourselves at personal risk on behalf of our brothers and sisters who are suffering.

One man who embodies this work is Pastor Edward, a Syrian man who still lives and works in Damascus despite the conflict in his country. For me, his commitment sums up the courage of surrendering one's whole life to Christ. Asked why he has chosen to stay rather than flee from the violence ripping his homeland apart, Pastor Edward says, "We are representing Christ, his heart, his love for people, and his holiness. There is a spiritual battle going on, and the powers of darkness are spreading. Killing people because 'they are not like me' is evil. So, as ambassadors of Christ, we will spread the values of heaven. Instead of revenge, forgiveness. Instead of hatred, love. Instead of killing, giving life. It's our responsibility to express those values even if we must pay a price." ➘

You can support Open Doors' work in the Middle East at opendoorsuk.org/SaveME.

Image courtesy of Alexandre Gallery, New York

As for Me

Northern Maine was my home
before I arrived.
It was what I was all about
all my life
even when I wasn't living here.
Someday
I will walk into the woods
and become an oak tree,
be cut down
and made into a cross.

Hanging On

He held to the Cross,
blood drops nourishing the earth.
Plant your garden here.

THOMAS LEQUIN

Above, Neil Welliver, *Sky in Cora's Marsh*, woodcut, 1986

The Chess Player

Ger Koopman

Illustrated by Christina Maendel

It was Christmas Eve. The whole day a cold wind had been blowing and now it had started to snow. Thousands – millions – of snowflakes came out of the sky and slowly covered the little village where Farmer Dyhema lived. They covered his fields, already plowed up for the next sowing; they covered his huge barns, full of hay or corn; they covered the yard, the big stable, and the house.

Old Farmer Dyhema had seen the snow coming down. He was sitting near the open fire in his easy chair. He liked the snow on his fields. It will make a better harvest next year, he thought. It was nice and warm in his room. On the table stood a chessboard. All the chessmen stood in their right places, four rows on the white and black squares of the board. Dyhema liked playing chess. He was waiting for the minister. Every Sunday evening the minister came to play chess with the old farmer, and also at Christmastime. He would come tonight. Oh, yes, Dyhema liked the game. He always won. There was nobody in the village who could play as well as he could. There was nobody

---

Geert "Ger" Koopman (1912–1983) was born in the Netherlands but after World War II moved to England, where he joined the Bruderhof community. Koopman wrote many stories, including this one, which was published in Home for Christmas *(Plough), and "The King and Death," published in* Easter Stories *(Plough).*

in the village who was as rich as he was. He was the best farmer, the richest farmer, the best chess player; and he was honest and righteous, too. He lived alone with his servants. His wife had died years ago. But this Christmas he was not thinking of his wife. He was always alone, thinking about himself. How good the harvest had been this year! What an important man he was in the village! When he walked through the streets they took their hats off as he passed. When somebody needed help – he gave it. When somebody needed work – he gave it. If anybody needed money – he lent it.

Suddenly the door opened. A servant came in. "It is rather late, Dyhema. Shall I keep the Christmas tart hot in the oven?"

Dyhema looked at the clock. "The minister is late," he said. "Yes, keep the tart hot."

The servant, moving toward the doorway, said, "I am afraid the minister will not come. The snow is very deep."

Dyhema looked cross, but he only said, "I can wait."

When the servant had gone, Dyhema stood up and looked out of the window. "Dear me, what a lot of snow," he said. "I am sure the minister will not come. The snow is very deep." Dyhema looked at the chessboard with longing eyes.

But somebody was coming! The Christ Child!

The whole day the Christ Child had been very busy. Christmas is his time, for then the hearts of people open, and that is what the Christ Child needs: open hearts. People think of their youth, how nice Christmas was at home. They think about their lives, and how things have turned out wrong. They long to change, to start anew. Then the Christ Child comes.

The whole day the Christ Child had been very busy. One thing had still to be done: to go to the old farmer, Dyhema. When God had told him that, he had said, "But his heart is not at all open." But God had only said, "Go. It has been closed and hard for too long. It is time now."

As the Christ Child was walking through the snow, he thought this over. What could he do? But when God says, "It is time," then it is time. And so at once the Christ Child was in the room of the old farmer. Nobody had heard him coming; nobody had seen him, but suddenly he was there. "Good evening, Dyhema," he said, in his beautiful voice.

Dyhema looked, and looked again. "Who are you, little boy, and how did you come in?"

The Christ Child sat down on a chair, opposite Dyhema, near the fire.

"I am the Christ Child."

"The Christ Child? So. What do you need?"

"I only want to talk to you."

"There is nothing to talk about. I did everything a man can do. I gave five hundred guilders for the Christmas celebration in the church."

"I know," said the Christ Child, "and two hundred and fifty guilders for the Sunday School celebration."

"Yes," said the farmer again, "and five hundred guilders for the poor people in the village; and wherever there are sick people, I send my servants to bring them a parcel."

"I know it all," said the Christ Child, and he sighed. "You are like a king on a throne who gives little presents to all his people. Yet how small these gifts are if you think of the thousands of guilders which you earned this year. And all these gifts were given, not out of love for others, but only out of love to yourself, so that you can sit here, content and satisfied with yourself. Oh, if you only knew the Christmas story!"

"I know it. By heart. 'In the days of the Emperor Augustus . . .'"

"See, you are quite wrong!"

"Wrong?" Farmer Dyhema took the Bible which was lying near him. "See, here it is. 'In the days of the Emperor Augustus . . .'"

"Wrong! I *know* the story. I am the Christ Child! It was not long, long ago, in the days of Augustus. It happens every year anew. Somewhere every year a child is born, poor and without clothes, waiting to be helped, by you. Sometimes it is a sick child, or a poor man, or a poor woman, waiting to be helped, by you. That is the Christmas story."

"I know that I am a sinner before God," said Dyhema. "Everyone is a sinner before God. But as far as I was able I did what I could. I cannot give all my money away, or anything like that. That is just nonsense."

"I do not ask only for money. I ask for much more than money. I ask for love! You said that you did everything you could? What about your daughter?"

The old farmer stood up angrily. "My daughter is dead. She is dead for me! If you were really the Christ Child you would know that ten years ago she married against my will. She married an artist, a musician, against my will. Children should obey their parents. No, do not speak about her."

"She is poor. She has a son."

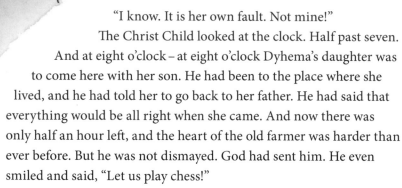

"I know. It is her own fault. Not mine!"

The Christ Child looked at the clock. Half past seven. And at eight o'clock – at eight o'clock Dyhema's daughter was to come here with her son. He had been to the place where she lived, and he had told her to go back to her father. He had said that everything would be all right when she came. And now there was only half an hour left, and the heart of the old farmer was harder than ever before. But he was not dismayed. God had sent him. He even smiled and said, "Let us play chess!"

"Can you play?"

"A little bit."

"Come on. That is better than all this talking."

They started. It seemed that the Christ Child was not a very good player. After ten minutes he had already lost two castles and a knight. Dyhema rubbed his hands. He would win the game. That was certain. When the Christ Child had lost nearly half his pieces, he suddenly spoke. "Imagine for a minute that your daughter came to you this Christmas Eve with your grandson. Would you receive them?"

"Stop that nonsense. Look at your game. You have nearly lost. And why should they come?"

"I have almost lost. Well, perhaps. But suppose I should win the game before eight o'clock, would you receive them?"

The old farmer laughed. "I would, because it is impossible."

The Christ Child smiled, too. It was one minute to eight. The Christ Child had only his king, queen, and one bishop. Dyhema had almost all his men. Dyhema looked at the clock. "Eight o'clock," he said.

"Eight o'clock. And I think it's checkmate," said the Christ Child.

"Checkmate?" Dyhema looked at the board. His eyes widened. "Oh? Wait a minute. You have changed the positions of all my men. No, no! But what has happened?"

The Christ Child smiled again. "That is what happens in life," he said. Then he looked very earnest. "Often people think they are lost. They think that nothing in the world can help them. And then God looks and says, 'It is time.' And all at once everything looks different. Everything comes into a different light, and all at once you see that all is not lost, but won. Remember this, Dyhema! All is not lost in his eyes. The lowly shall be lifted up – the first shall be last." And then he was gone.

Dyhema stood up. He sat down in his chair near the fire. He closed his eyes. He would think this over.

Suddenly he awoke. Somebody had knocked at the door. He rubbed his eyes. I have been sleeping, he thought. I had a wonderful dream about the Christ Child. He looked at the table. There was the chessboard. The two rows of white men and the two rows of black men stood neatly on opposite sides of the board. Yes, it had been a dream. "Come in," he said. A servant came in.

"Dyhema, here is a little boy. He says . . . "

Dyhema stood up in astonishment. "A little boy with his mother?"

"No, he is alone. But he says his mother had an accident. She has sprained her ankle. She is waiting in the snow about half a mile away. She sent the boy for help."

Dyhema laughed. He thought, of course it is not my daughter. And then he said, "Send the servants out with the horse and cart. Make a room ready and bring her here. Send for the doctor. Bring the boy here."

The servant went out. A moment later a boy of about nine came in. Dyhema stood up. He was strangely moved. The boy looked – yes, he looked just as he himself must have looked long, long ago. "What is your name?"

"Sigurd," said the boy.

Dyhema sank back into his chair. He closed his eyes. Sigurd, that was his name. His daughter had called her son after him. But what about the Christ Child? It was a dream, of course. But dreams are lies, nonsense. But still, there was the boy. His grandson. No. He would not receive his daughter. He stood up and went to the kitchen. Only one old servant was there. "Where are the others?" he asked.

"They are all with their families, of course, and two have gone out to fetch the poor woman," she said.

"I do not want her here! They must take her somewhere else!"

"Dyhema! On Christmas Eve you are going to refuse a poor woman your house! Very well. You are responsible. But I cannot go out and through the snow. Who will tell them?"

"As soon as they are here, call me. But don't let the woman come into the house."

Dyhema went back to the living room. The boy sat near the fireplace. When Dyhema came in he stood up and, going to him, the boy said, "Are you my grandfather?"

"Of course not," Dyhema said angrily.

The boy looked sad. "Then I have come to the wrong farm. You know, Mummy said, when she fell down, 'That light over there is the farm. Run over there and ask for help.' But it does not matter. When Mummy comes here

she can tell you where she wanted to go. She was born in this village, you know. My granddad is the richest farmer in the village. My mummy said, 'He is like a little king. Everyone asks for his advice. He is very clever, you know.'"

Dyhema suddenly said, "Why are you going to your grandfather?"

"Mummy said that the Christ Child had told her to go. We have never been there. We are very poor, you know. My daddy is dead. We had no money, but Mummy always said, 'I will not take the first step.' And then all at once she told me that the Christ Child had told her to go."

"Did she see the Christ Child?"

"I don't know. Afterwards she said it was a dream. And on the journey she was very uncertain. She said to me, once, 'Do not be surprised if we only stay for a short time.'"

Dyhema said nothing. He looked into the fire. Suddenly the boy saw the chessboard. He went to the table. "My granddad can play chess! He always wins, my mummy says! Can you play? I can. Mummy says that I play so well because I got it from my granddad. Shall we play? Do you know, I am hungry. We had no supper."

Dyhema looked up. "Can you really play? Such a small child?"

"I am not small. And I often win."

"Come on, let us try," Dyhema said.

After a short time Dyhema understood that the boy really could play. Almost without thinking he made the right moves. After half an hour Dyhema became restless. The boy was winning! Really, the small boy seemed to be a better player than he was. And what annoyed him most was that while he did his utmost to win, the boy just played, without thinking it over. If Dyhema made a move, after a long time of consideration, the boy followed immediately, and it was always the right move. Perhaps it was because Dyhema was so annoyed that he suddenly made a wrong move. The boy smiled. "That is a bad move," he said. "You had better take it back."

"No, what I have done, I have done!"

The boy looked at him. Why was this old man so angry? He could not help it, could he? Was it because he could not win the game? A lot of people grew angry if they could not win. It was interesting. You learned most in a game that you lost. But this was an old man. Perhaps . . .

Suddenly the old servant came in. "Dyhema, what about the Christmas tart? Can I bring it in now?"

Dyhema looked very angry. "Go away with your tart!"

What a pity, the boy thought. He was so hungry. How angry the old man

was. Was that only because he was not winning? Suddenly he said, "I should like to have some tart. I had no supper, you know."

Dyhema only said, "Your turn to play."

Sigurd sighed. Then he had an idea. He would let the old man win. He would make a bad move. It was not easy to do that. He sighed. It is Christmas Eve, he thought, I will do it. And he made his move.

Dyhema laughed. "A bad move. See, I can take your queen. Oh, I knew I could win. I have never yet lost a game!"

Sigurd blushed. This was not fair. He had always been told not to be sad if he lost, and not to be proud if he won. Suddenly he smiled. If I can cheer him up, let him win, he thought, and he said, "You can never be sure who wins before it is checkmate."

All the time Dyhema had looked at the boy. He had seen the tears come into his eyes after he had spoken. And he had seen the change, the smile. And then the words of the boy. It was as if he saw the Christ Child again. He remembered the words of the Christ Child, "Sometimes you think all is lost." He stood up. He walked up and down the room. The boy looked at him in surprise. Dyhema saw his life – his long life – in a new light. No mistakes? Open and right? There was a fault, a great fault. How could he have been so blind? My heart has been cold and unmoved, yet I've always thought I was such a good man, with all my good deeds. What a wretched old man I am. All this he felt deep in his heart and he saw his dream again, heard the words of the Christ Child, "God comes. He brings something new into life. *Love!*" That was it. Love!

Dyhema went to the boy. He put his hand on his shoulder. "You have won," he said, "you and the Christ Child."

The boy looked up at him in astonishment. "What do you mean?"

Old Farmer Dyhema smiled. "It does not matter, my son," he said. "It does not matter. But remember this: the Christ Child brings new life, yet all seemed so lost to man when Jesus was born. Born in a stable, poor and cold. All seemed to have been utterly lost in the end, my son. A cross was the end. We must remember, Sigurd, remember the moment when God looked and said, 'It is the time.' And it was! The cross was not the end. And even today the Christ Child still comes to warm the hearts of men."

There was a hard knocking, and the door opened. The old servant said, "Tell me, Dyhema, where must I send this woman? She is here now."

"Bring her in here, of course."

"But you said . . . "

"It is my daughter! Didn't you know that? Bring her in here at once! Quick! And bring the Christmas tart. Quick, it is Christmas!" ➤

Image courtesy of Bowdoin College Museum of Art

Testimony

Fisher, marten and coyote pelts
hang from my camp walls.

Whitetail deer, you stare at me,
elk horns of Colorado
point me out.

You gather in testimony on the pine
walls – for or against?

"Hunt me some game," said my father,
"that I may bless you." *

THOMAS LEQUIN
* Gen. 27:4–5

Above, Neil Welliver, *Deer in Bottom,* painting, 1980

Editors' Picks

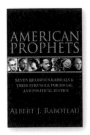

American Prophets
Albert J. Raboteau
(Princeton University Press)

What good does religion do in politics? Here's an answer. This excellent introduction to the lives of seven truly prophetic voices of the last century shows how their boldness, love for humanity, and willingness to suffer stemmed from a deep personal relationship with the living God, which burned "like fire in the bones" (Jer. 20:9).

One can't do justice to any of these figures in a chapter, but religious scholar Raboteau gets quickly to the heart of their witness, outlining the stories and spiritual insight of Abraham Joshua Heschel, Thomas Merton, Howard Thurman, Dorothy Day, A. J. Muste, Martin Luther King Jr., and Fannie Lou Hamer.

Raboteau traces the close connections between these men and women, who learned much from each other. They raised their voices together at a *kairos* moment; the time was ripe for the prophetic vision of a few to move millions to self-sacrificial action out of love to others.

Surely we're due for another such moment. Rather than bemoan the dearth of prophetic voices today, we can follow the same call. As Heschel insists: "This world, this society can be redeemed. God has a stake in our moral predicament. I cannot believe that God will be defeated."

Hacksaw Ridge
Film directed by Mel Gibson

We wondered how Desmond Doss, the first conscientious objector to win a Congressional Medal of Honor, would survive the Hollywood treatment. The protagonist of Mel Gibson's new film refuses to carry a gun and goes on to save seventy-five men as a medic during the battle of Okinawa.

A *Chicago Tribune* review calling the film "the most bloodthirsty movie about a pacifist ever made" is on point; war really is hell, but we don't need Mel Gibson to teach us that. The most thought-provoking parts of the film occur off the battlefield: Doss's relationship with his girlfriend (and later wife), his repeated clashes with military brass and fellow soldiers, and the formative influence of his father, a deeply damaged World War I veteran who presented young Doss with an illustrated copy of the Ten Commandments depicting Cain killing his brother Abel. Doss later said, "I wondered, How in the world could a brother do such a thing? It put a horror in my heart of just killing, and as a result I took it personally: 'Desmond, if you love me, you won't kill.'"

Doss's religious conviction was perceived as unmanly cowardice, a sign of feeble character. But what defines courage? It's not all hard-bitten muscle and smoking firepower. What about moral bravery, the strength to stand alone for what you believe is right? It won't make you popular and is harder to attain, but will almost certainly have more enduring consequences. Through his actions Doss disproved his naysayers, even as he saved their lives. ⬩ *The Editors*

INSIGHT

JOHN F. KENNEDY

War will exist until that distant day when the conscientious objector enjoys the same reputation and prestige that the warrior does today.

Source: Letter to a Navy friend, quoted in Arthur M. Schlesinger, Jr., *A Thousand Days: John F. Kennedy in the White House* (Houghton Mifflin, 1965), 88.

Can Society Be Christian?

Reviving T. S. Eliot's Vision

NATHANIEL PETERS

IN A PLURALISTIC WORLD that views traditional faith with suspicion, what would a Christian society look like? What should Christians hope for their countries? R. R. Reno, editor of *First Things,* asks this question in his new book, *Resurrecting the Idea of a Christian Society.* He borrows his title from T. S. Eliot's "The Idea of a Christian Society," an essay based on a series of lectures Eliot delivered in 1939, six months before Britain and Germany went to war. Eliot's writing is marked by the shadow of hostility and unrest. It's a feeling we have come to know in our own time: the uncertainty of imminent, unknown change. Eliot's essay is loftier and more formal, while Reno's book is grittier and more connected to the present struggles Christians face. They are worth reading together as we try to understand where we are and what we should do as Christians in post-Christian societies.

In the 1930s, many Americans and Britons called their societies Christian, largely to distinguish themselves from the barbarities of Nazi Germany and the Soviet Union. For Eliot, that was not enough. He argues that the "idea" of a society is the end toward which it is ordered and the deep structure of its thought and culture. A Christian society, then, is "not the same thing as a society consisting exclusively of devout Christians. It would be a society in which the natural end of man – virtue and well-being in community – is acknowledged for all, and the supernatural end – beatitude – for those who have the eyes to see it."

However, that no longer described the Britain in which Eliot lived. Despite talk of the nation as a Christian society, Eliot thought that his nation was in "a kind of doldrums between opposing winds of doctrine, in a period in which one political philosophy has lost its cogency for behavior, though it is still the only one in which public speech can be framed." Britain was stuck between a positive culture, Christianity, and a negative one, rebellion against Christianity. More and more people were turning away from the Christian faith, but they lacked something of real substance with which to replace it. Eliot saw this lukewarm middle ground as closer to paganism than full-blooded Christian faith. He predicted that British society would continue in these doldrums and proceed into a gradual decline unless it took either a positive secular shape or a positive Christian one.

If Britain did not rebuild its Christian foundation, and if secular liberalism continued its rise, Eliot predicted that standards for art and culture would suffer. He also thought that the common bonds of society would begin to fray.

Nathaniel Peters is a doctoral candidate in historical theology at Boston College.

Image from the Smithsonian American Art Museum

"The Liberal notion that religion was a matter of private belief and of conduct in private life, and that there is no reason why Christians should not be able to accommodate themselves to any world which treats them good-naturedly, is becoming less and less tenable," he wrote. "The reason why members of different communions have been able to rub along together is that in the greater part of the ordinary business of life they have shared the same assumptions about behavior."

This is part of Eliot's argument that Christians should not simply claim the freedom to worship as they please and suffer no harm to their faith. Rather, they should

William H. Johnson, *Church on Lenox Avenue*

strive for a society whose instincts and goals are Christian: "The Christian can be satisfied with nothing less than a Christian organization of society." This does not entail the criminalization of other religions or the persecution of nonbelievers. Rather, it means that Christians should strive to have a society in which the things we hold in common – despite our pluralism – are Christian things. Christians will flourish much more in a pluralistic society that forbids wife-beating and widow-burning because of the dignity of the human person – a concept derived from Christianity but not exclusive to it – than in one that allows these acts on religious grounds.

Seventy-seven years later, on both sides of the Atlantic, we can see just how many of

Eliot's prophecies have come to pass. Secular liberalism has not only continued to erode the Christian cultural foundation of our societies, but has begun to replace it with its own. The Christian assumptions that once united the various elements in our pluralistic societies have broken down, leaving us less civil toward one another. We are more free to do what we want, but less sure that what we want will actually make us happy or good. We speak of our society not as pagan but as post-Christian – a continued rebellion against one deep structure rather than an adherence to a robust replacement. As the disease has progressed, its symptoms have become more extreme.

But what about Eliot's diagnosis? To begin with, Eliot was clear that his thoughts would require modification for application outside of Britain. He assumed a relatively uniform society with an established church, not the pluralism of the globalized West. Nonetheless, he identifies three elements that remain necessary for Christians anywhere to form their society.

The first of these is education. Eliot saw education as essential to the foundation of a society: "A nation's system of education is much more important than its system of government; only a proper system of education can unify the active and the contemplative life, action and speculation, politics and the arts." The purpose of education, then, is not to impart information for the sake of a career or citizenship, but to form a moral foundation for one's life.

This holistic formation should be the goal of Christian education, too, in homes and Christian schools. Christian education is not simply a project to make men and women pious Christians, but to "train people to be able to think in Christian categories." Beauty is not just the gratification of contemporary tastes, but a reflection of the order and symmetry God inscribed in the world. Riches are not God's blessing to you for your personal use; you hold them in trust for the benefit of others in your church and community. Thinking in Christian categories instead of simply giving worldly ones the veneer of faith leads to authentically Christian lives – and thereby, ever so slowly, to authentically Christian societies.

Second, Eliot says that a society that would be Christian needs a "community of Christians." This is not an organization or a particular caste but "a body of indefinite outline; composed of both clergy and laity, of the more conscious, more spiritually and intellectually developed of both. It will be their identity of belief and aspiration, their background of a common system of education and a common culture, which will enable them to influence and be influenced by each other, and collectively to form the conscious mind and the conscience of the nation." In other words, the Christian renewal of society will need a critical mass of those who think and live according to authentically Christian principles and categories. These Christians need to talk to each other, to inquire into the truth, to bring their families together over dinner. They need to determine and cling to what they hold in common as Christians, despite the real differences they have. They must commit to living and thinking according to Christ's "more excellent way."

> The secular reformer conceives of the evils of the world as something outside himself. The Christian, by contrast, must see them within.

Third, this will automatically entail humility and conversion of self before conversion of society. Eliot's lectures were provoked by a letter he read in the *Times* (London) from J. H. Oldham, the Scottish missionary who was part of the same roundtable of Christian thinkers. In the letter, Oldham writes: "To focus our attention on evil in others is a way of escape from the painful struggle of eradicating it from our own hearts and lives and an evasion of our real responsibilities." Eliot saw this as one of the great differences between secular and Christian reformers. The secular reformer conceives of the evils of the world as something outside himself. The Christian, by contrast, must see them within. He himself must be converted along with the rest of the world and is deprived of the exhilaration of only seeing an external enemy. To forget this is to fall into a pride that would poison our efforts.

In his book, Reno does not emphasize education or our own pursuit of the virtues to the same degree. When he does talk about education, it is in the context of America's post-Christian elite destroying the moral fabric our society needs: "The most pressing social justice issue today is the moral exploitation of the poor and vulnerable by the well-off and powerful, an exploitation masked by the rhetoric of liberation." The deregulation of our morality has had far greater social effects than the deregulation of our markets. The task of renewing society lies with ordinary believers who can provide that missing moral regulation. They should dare to disapprove. Reno therefore calls for "judgmentalism," by which he means "the courage to speak forthrightly about right and wrong."

At the heart of that moralism must lie a Christian understanding of freedom. As Eliot noted, Christians must use Christian principles to structure their thought and action. Christians must understand freedom not as the ability to do whatever we want and to define ourselves however we will, but as the flourishing that comes from obeying the law of God. It is in serving God that we are freed from the captivity of our own desires. It is in dying to ourselves that we find life.

This kind of freedom is not sought alone. It is found in, and strengthens, the community we need in order to have rich, meaningful lives. That kind of social solidarity should come through subsidiarity, Reno argues, the idea that social action should take place at the appropriate level of society. The state should not seek to replace churches, clubs, businesses, and families in their important social roles. Subsidiarity promotes human dignity, he argues, "because it encourages a thick local culture that encourages our free, responsible

Piet Mondrian, *Sun, Church in Zeeland*

Image from the Tate Modern Art Gallery, London

participation." And the institutions most important and in greatest need of strengthening are churches and families.

Even though American society may be more unabashedly secular than Eliot's Britain was, Reno sees post-Christian America as dissatisfied with its mores. Rich or poor, we all want decency and dignity, and to give ourselves in love to our spouse, our loved ones, and God. The time is ripe to propose the truths of our faith again. Twenty-five percent of Americans attend church weekly, a number that has remained the same for decades. This is the committed core from which Reno thinks we can begin our rebuilding efforts, the community of Christians that can leaven our society. The numbers may be smaller in Europe, but the hunger for renewal is no less real.

Perhaps most importantly, Eliot reminds us that we cannot build Christian societies by sacrificing Christian principles to elect unchristian politicians. Nor can we pursue a Christian society without remembering that we ourselves need to be reformed. Rather, "only in humility, charity, and purity – and most of all perhaps humility – can we be prepared to receive the grace of God without which human operations are vain." ➤

Joe Strummer

JASON LANDSEL

"This is a public service announcement – with guitars!" Left knee energetically pumping, black Fender Telecaster in hand, Joe Strummer called audiences worldwide to attention. This was "Combat Rock."

This year marks four decades since the celebrated UK punk band The Clash formed in 1976. Despite the passage of time, their mutinous snarls, rebellious spirit, and global vision still resonate today, acting as an atomic alarm clock alerting sleepers everywhere to wake up and get to work. Touted as "the only band that matters," they sought to change the world through a musical insurrection. In some ways, they succeeded.

For many, stumbling upon The Clash was transformational. Their songs spoke bluntly against fascism, racism, and brutality; they critiqued capitalist corruption. They left listeners feeling: no, we don't have to submissively take this abuse, the future is still to be written, and we can somehow be part of it.

Joe Strummer, The Clash's front man, was born John Graham Mellor in 1952. He lived in various countries as a child, thanks to his father's career as a British foreign service diplomat. As a young man, after art school, he worked as a janitor, gravedigger, ukulele-strumming busker in the London Underground, and a member of a rockabilly band, where his unique playing style earned him the name "Strummer."

> "Punk rock means exemplary manners to your fellow human being."
>
> Joe Strummer

The tumultuous social, political, and economic climate of 1970s England unbolted the door for a punk eruption. Punk made audible the inexpressible; with only a few chords and a lot of volume it transformed widespread dissatisfaction into sound. Formed in the midst of this movement, The Clash recorded and toured almost unceasingly. Their albums *London Calling* and *Combat Rock* embody some of their best work.

Though the band members eventually parted ways, in the years that followed Joe Strummer held fast to his ideals, no matter how out of step with the times they seemed.

> I'd like to say that people can change anything they want to; and that means everything in the world. Show me any country and there'll be people in it. And it's the people that make the country. People have got to stop pretending they're not on the world. People are running about following their little tracks. I am one of them. But we've all gotta just stop following our own little mouse trail. People are out there doing bad things to each other. . . . Greed . . . it ain't going anywhere! They should have that on a big billboard across Times Square. Think on that. Without people, you're nothing.

In a world where walls and differences are emphasized and even encouraged, his message of unification remains as relevant as ever. In his own words, "Punk ain't the boots or the hair dye. It must be the attitude that you have, that [you] approach everything in life with that attitude. . . . In fact, punk rock means exemplary manners to your fellow human being." ⤳

Jason Landsel is the artist for Plough's *"Forerunners" series, including the painting opposite.*